COOKING WITH *More* CONFIDENCE

Inspirations for Good Food at Home

To April ~
So nice to meet you!
Have fun in your kitchen ~
always ~

Eunice Naomi Wiebolt
03
2018

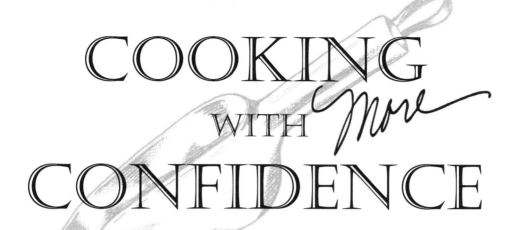

COOKING
WITH *More*
CONFIDENCE

Inspirations for Good Food at Home

Eunice Naomi Wiebolt

Tony Martin Photography

ROMARIN PUBLISHING CO.
Minnesota

Romarin Publishing Co.
1945 Red Oak Drive SW
Brainerd, MN 56401
romarin@scicable.com

Book design by Eunice Naomi Wiebolt
Photographs by Tony Martin
Original Drawings by Amanda Dorholt
Graphic Design/Project Coordinator - Kelly S. Dorholt
Editor - David D. Dorholt

Printed in the United States of America by Bang Printing

Library of Congress Cataloging-In-Publication Data:

Wiebolt, Eunice Naomi.
Cooking with more confidence : inspirations for good food at home /
Eunice Naomi Wiebolt ; Tony Martin Photography.
p. cm.
Includes index.

LCCN 2016958768
ISBN 0-9718894-2-2

0-9718894-2-2
10 9 8 7 6 5 4 3 2 1
First Edition

Cover: Lemon Cheesecake, page 171
Back Cover: Pork with Roasted Grapes, page 138
Crunchy Granola, page 41

Dedication

Cooking with More Confidence is
dedicated with love to my sons,
daughters-in-law, and grandchildren,

along with friends across the country
who have blessed me with their wonderful
love and support;

to my brothers and sisters, and
to the memory of those so dear
who have gone before us.

Eunice Naomi Wiebolt

Acknowledgments

Special and Sincere Thanks

to Kelly Dorholt for being the
Project Coordinator and Graphic Designer

to David Dorholt for being the Editor

to Amanda Dorholt for her original artwork gracing
the pages of this book

to Emma Dorholt, Kelly Dorholt, and Rae Skinner
for being my food assistants during the photography sessions

to Pat Birznieks, Sherry Johnson, Karen Kreiser, Bridget Lindner,
Jan Sheets, and Jani Wiebolt for their critical recipe testing

and to family members and friends for their ever-so-patient
anticipation, encouragement, and tastings. I couldn't have
done this without you, and will be forever grateful.

Eunice Naomi Wiebolt

Table of Contents

Introduction

COOKING WITH MORE CONFIDENCE

Those who have many fingerprints on the cover of my first book know I am an enthusiastic proponent of sharing good food - whether that means meals with your family, an impromptu get together with friends, or simply appreciating a quiet evening at home.

Food comforts, sustains, and renews our daily lives. We are so fortunate to live in this great country where ingredients are readily available to stock our kitchen pantries. I am grateful to people who plant. People who have gardens. People who bring their goods to a market. People who run our grocery stores. People who farm, and take the risk every single year that cooperating weather conditions will help raise a decent crop.

Love of good food begins at home and lasts a lifetime. Our challenge is to return to the kitchen. Let us look at each other, talk to each other, and cook with each other. Let us take our family and ourselves from just getting by at mealtime to creating our own food experiences. Without a doubt, positive reinforcement turns an aspiration into inspiration. I encourage you to share good food and make lasting memories with those you care about. Use this book to help you.

Significant life skills of communication, appreciation, cooperation and attention to detail are honed to a fine edge in the kitchen. These recipes will work for one set of hands or many. Please enjoy this cookbook, and share the journey and love along the way.

COOKING
WITH *More*
CONFIDENCE

Inspirations for Good Food at Home

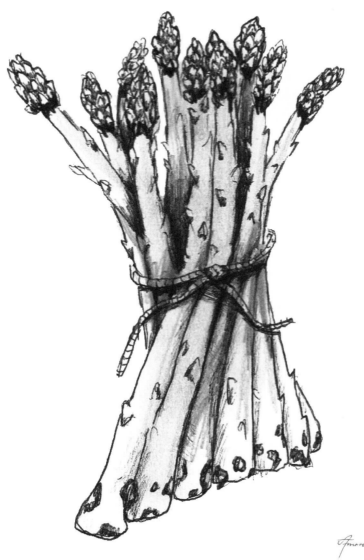

Asparagus officinalus

(asparagus)

Starters

Asparagus Rollups
Bacon Jam
Chicken Mini Meatballs
Cranberry Cheese Log
Crostini Gone Crazy
Cucumber Yogurt Dip
Delicious Mushroom Spread
Easy Tortilla Toasts
Guacamole
Ham and Cheese Mini Biscuits
Mediterranean Olive Spread
The Nut Page
Oven Roasted Shrimp
Parmesan Bread Dip
Reuben Bites on Rye
Smashed Potato Appetizer
Stuffed Mushrooms
Triple Onion Bacon Dip
Warm Marinated Olives

Scoops of Confidence

COOKING with MORE CONFIDENCE

Asparagus Rollups

6-8 servings

A crunchy and creamy delight, these will give you a great start to your culinary journey.

24 thin asparagus spears
1 teaspoon kosher salt
1 teaspoon granulated sugar
8 slices lean bacon, finely chopped
12 slices white sandwich bread
1 8-ounce package cream cheese, room temperature
1/2 teaspoon dry mustard
2 tablespoons green onions, very finely chopped
4 tablespoons butter, melted

Preheat oven to 400 degrees. Line a rimmed baking sheet with parchment; set aside.

Cut asparagus spears to a 5-inch length. Bring water to a boil in a medium saucepan; add salt and sugar. Add asparagus; cook 1 1/2 minutes until crisp-tender. Drain; immediately plunge into ice cold water to stop the cooking. When asparagus is totally cold, transfer to a paper towel to dry completely.

Cook and stir bacon pieces in a skillet over medium heat about 3 minutes until crispy. Using a slotted spoon, transfer cooked bacon from the pan to a paper towel to drain and cool.

Stack up slices of bread and cut off the crusts. Flatten each slice of bread with a rolling pin; set aside. Combine cream cheese, mustard, onions, and bacon pieces. Spread each flattened slice of bread with about 2 tablespoons of the cream cheese mixture, covering its surface completely.

Place 2 asparagus spears on the wide end of each bread piece and roll it up. Transfer rolls to a cutting board. Cut each roll into equal-sized pieces; dip in melted butter. Place, seam side down, on prepared pan. Bake 15 minutes until rolls are lightly browned. Serve warm.

If made ahead, refrigerate in an airtight glass container. Re-warm by baking 10-12 minutes in a preheated 325 degree oven.

Bacon Jam

Bacon lovers rejoice! It's savory. It's sweet. Make this jam for your foodie friends - they will love you so much more. Guaranteed. Try to resist the urge to eat this with a spoon.

1 1/2 pounds lean bacon, cut in small pieces
1 cup onions, chopped
4 large cloves garlic, chopped
1 teaspoon chili powder
1/2 teaspoon dried ginger
1/2 teaspoon dry mustard
1 1/2 teaspoons hot sauce
1/2 cup fine Kentucky whiskey
1/4 cup pure maple syrup
1/3 cup light brown sugar, packed
2 tablespoons dry sherry
4 tablespoons balsamic vinegar

Fry bacon in a skillet over medium heat until it is cooked through but NOT crispy. Transfer cooked bacon to paper towels to drain. Reserve 2 tablespoons of bacon fat in the pan. Add onions to the skillet; cook and stir 5 minutes over medium heat. Add garlic; cook an additional minute. Return bacon pieces to the skillet. Reduce heat. Add remaining ingredients; simmer 30 minutes, stirring occasionally. (This extra cooking time will reduce the mixture to a thick, syrupy consistency.) Cool 20-25 minutes. Transfer mixture to a food processor. Pulse several times, blending to a thick jam.

Now let your imagination soar to new heights. Here are a few ideas to get you started:
Serve on plain crostini, use on a grilled cheese sandwich - or in place of bacon on a bacon, lettuce, and tomato sandwich, add to scrambled eggs, mix a little into alfredo sauce and serve with pasta, add to a burger, spoon into mashed potatoes, mix with roasted red potatoes, or use as a base for a warm bacon salad dressing.

Jam may be refrigerated in a glass, airtight container for 7 days - or frozen up to 1 month.

Chicken Mini Meatballs

Makes 30 meatballs

You will make these again and again. I would encourage you to grind your own chicken, thereby controlling the amount of light meat for bulk and dark meat for flavor.

1 1/2 pounds chicken (breast and thighs) to equal 2 1/2 cups ground
1 cup panko bread crumbs
1/2 cup milk
1 egg, lightly beaten
2 teaspoons fresh garlic, minced
3/4 teaspoon kosher salt
1/2 teaspoon freshly ground black pepper
1/2 cup onions, finely chopped
2 tablespoons low-sodium soy sauce
1 tablespoon fresh flat leaf parsley, minced

Preheat oven to 425 degrees. Lightly coat mini muffin tins with non-stick cooking spray. Line a rimmed baking sheet with foil; transfer the prepared muffin tins to the pan, and set aside.

Cut chicken in small pieces; freeze until semi-hard - they will be much easier to handle. Grind in a food processor, a few pieces at a time. Mix bread crumbs with milk; let rest for 2-3 minutes to soften. Combine softened crumbs with egg, garlic, salt, pepper, onions, soy sauce and parsley; mix well.

Add crumb mixture to ground chicken; use a fork to gently combine all ingredients. Fill muffin tins to the top. Bake 25-30 minutes until tops are browned and meatballs are bubbly. Let rest in the pans for 5 minutes; add your favorite barbeque sauce to coat well. Transfer to a serving platter; serve with toothpicks.

Variations: For an Asian flavor, add 2 teaspoons fresh lemon juice and 2 teaspoons grated fresh ginger.
Serve with Orange Dipping Sauce (recipe, page 117).
For Italian flavor, add 2 teaspoons oregano, 1/2 teaspoon red pepper flakes; roll in grated
Parmesan cheese. Serve with your favorite marinara sauce.

Cranberry Cheese Log

8-10 servings

Colorful and tasty, this is a super-easy appetizer.

1 8-ounce package cream cheese, room temperature
3/4 cup blue cheese, crumbled
1/2 cup feta cheese, crumbled
1/2 cup dried cranberries, finely chopped
3/4 cup pecans, toasted and finely chopped
crackers of your choice for serving

In a food processor (or by hand), thoroughly combine all three cheeses. Add cranberry pieces; mix well to distribute evenly. Spoon cheese mixture onto a sheet of plastic wrap. Using your hands, form a log shape about 8 inches in length. Wrap tightly; refrigerate until firm. Remove plastic wrap; re-wrap tightly with foil and place in freezer.

Toast pecans in a dry skillet over medium low heat; stir constantly for 2-3 minutes until they are fragrant and slightly browned. After they have cooled completely, chop and set aside.

To finish, unwrap log from foil; defrost slightly in refrigerator. Coat the cheese log with pecans, gently pressing them onto the surface. Place on a serving dish. Allow the cheese log to stand at room temperature for about 30 minutes to come to a spreadable consistency. Serve with crackers.

Crostini Gone Crazy

Who doesn't need a little crazy? Terrific variations on one easy base.

Basic Recipe for Crostini:

Preheat oven to 375 degrees. Cut 1/2-inch slices from a French baguette. Brush lightly with good olive oil. Bake 12-14 minutes. Edges should be brown. Bottoms should be soft.

Crostini with Gruyère and Wine Jelly

Top thin crostini with a sliver of Gruyère cheese and a dollop of Wine Jelly.

Wine Jelly:
3 cups granulated sugar
2 cups Zinfandel or other full-bodied, jammy, red wine
3 ounces liquid fruit pectin

Combine sugar and wine in top of a double boiler over simmering water.
Stir about 3 minutes or until all the sugar dissolves. Add pectin; stir constantly for 1 minute.
Remove from heat. Skim off any foam that may have formed on top of the jelly.
Fill sterilized glass jelly jars within 1 inch of the top; seal.

Crostini with Goat Cheese and Olive Tapenade

Spread crostini with a teaspoon of goat cheese; top with a small amount of Olive Tapenade.

Olive Tapenade:
1 tablespoon good olive oil
1 cup kalamata olives, pitted and well drained
1 large clove garlic, minced
1 tablespoon capers, rinsed and drained
1/4 cup Italian flat parsley (leaves only), finely chopped
2 tablespoons fresh lime juice
1 teaspoon white wine vinegar
1/4 teaspoon freshly ground black pepper

Heat oil in a small skillet over medium heat. Add olives and garlic; cook and stir 2 minutes.
Place olive mixture and all remaining ingredients in a small food processor; pulse
until smooth.

Cucumber Yogurt Dip

Makes 2 cups

A fresh and full flavored do-ahead treat for your appetizer table. I also rely on this to be a creative accompaniment to grilled fish, vegetables, or baked potatoes.

1 1/2 cups plain yogurt, drained*
1/2 English cucumber, unpeeled and grated to equal 1 cup
1 1/2 teaspoons kosher salt
1/4 cup sour cream
1 1/2 teaspoons grated lemon rind
1 tablespoon fresh lemon juice
1 large clove fresh, minced garlic
1 tablespoon green onion, very finely sliced
1 teaspoon fresh dill (or 1 tablespoon dried dill weed)
2 teaspoons white wine vinegar
1/4 teaspoon white pepper
3 pita rounds, cut in 8 wedges
1 teaspoon good olive oil

* Drain all possible liquid from the yogurt. This is best done one day before you wish to serve the dip. For this task, the easiest method is to place a round paper coffee filter inside a fine mesh strainer and set the strainer over a small, deep bowl. Spoon yogurt into the filter. Cover bowl and strainer completely with plastic wrap, and refrigerate for a few hours or overnight. Discard the excess liquid. At least two hours before completing the dip, place the grated cucumber and salt in a small bowl; cover, and refrigerate (this process will draw moisture from the cucumber).

To assemble, combine the drained yogurt, sour cream, lemon rind, lemon juice, garlic, onion, dill, vinegar, and pepper in a medium bowl; mix thoroughly. Using paper towels, squeeze **all** the excess water from the grated cucumber. It should feel quite dry to the touch. Add cucumber to the yogurt mixture; blend well.

Preheat oven to 400 degrees. Place pita wedges on a baking sheet; brush both sides with olive oil. Bake 5 minutes, flip the wedges over, and bake additional 5 minutes. Serve warm or at room temperature with dip. Any left over should be covered, refrigerated, and used within 2 days.

COOKING with MORE CONFIDENCE

Delicious Mushroom Spread

Makes about 2 1/2 cups

The earthy depth of flavors will exceed your expectations.

2 teaspoons good olive oil
8 ounces fresh button mushrooms, cleaned and diced
1/2 cup shallots, diced
2 large cloves fresh garlic, minced
1 tablespoon balsamic vinegar
1 teaspoon low-sodium soy sauce
1/2 teaspoon onion powder
1/4 teaspoon kosher salt
1/8 teaspoon coarsely ground black pepper
1 8-ounce package cream cheese, room temperature
1/4 cup sun-dried tomatoes in oil, drained and finely diced

Heat oil in a skillet over medium heat. Add mushrooms; cook and stir over medium heat about 4-5 minutes until mushrooms begin to release their liquid. Increase heat; cook and stir additional few minutes until all the liquid has evaporated. Reduce heat. Add shallots; cook another 2 minutes. Add garlic and cook 1 minute. Add vinegar, soy sauce, onion powder, salt, and pepper; cook an additional minute to blend flavors. Remove from heat and set aside to cool.

Beat cream cheese until smooth; stir in cooled mushroom mixture and diced tomatoes.

Spoon into a serving dish; serve at room temperature with crostini (recipe, page 21) or mild crackers.

Easy Tortilla Toasts

24 wedges

Your habit of reaching for plain tortilla chips is about to be diminished. Put these on a plate and they'll be gone in seconds. So much better than chips and cheese.

3 12-inch flour tortillas
1/2 cup butter, melted
2 tablespoons canola oil
1 1/2 cups shredded sharp cheddar cheese
1 1/2 cups shredded Monterey Jack cheese
Optional Toppings: sliced green onions, pepperoni, sliced olives, green chiles

Line 2 large, rimmed baking sheets with parchment; set aside.
Stack tortillas on top of one another. Using a pizza cutter, cut into 8 wedges. Melt butter and oil together in a large skillet. Submerge tortilla wedges in to the butter and oil mixture; make sure each one is covered. Let them rest 30 minutes to soften.

Preheat oven to 400 degrees.

Remove tortilla wedges from the butter and oil mixture; transfer to prepared pans. Bake 10 minutes until crisp and bubbly. Turn the oven heat off. Mix the 2 cheeses; distribute evenly on wedges. Return pans to the oven for 2 minutes to melt cheese. Decorate with toppings of your choice. Pop the wedges back into the oven for a minute or two if your topping (such as pepperoni*) tastes better hot.

Serve warm or at room temperature. Any butter left over from the softening process can certainly be used to make another batch.

*Sometimes pepperoni seems a bit oily. Solution? Drop the slices in boiling water for about 30 seconds; remove from water, and blot dry before using as usual.

Guacamole

An avocado evolution. Taste the difference homemade makes.

5 ripe avocados
4 tablespoons fresh lime juice
2/3 cup red onion, finely diced
1 large clove garlic, minced
1 teaspoon kosher salt
3/4 teaspoon coarsely ground black pepper
1 1/2 cups fresh Roma tomatoes, seeded and finely diced*
1 tablespoon hot sauce (or to taste)
1/2 cup fresh cilantro, chopped (optional)

Cut avocados in half and remove the pits. Using a sharp paring knife, cut through the flesh vertically and horizontally to cube. Remove avocado from its shell with a spoon, and place in a large bowl. Mash lightly. Immediately mix in lime juice to brighten the flavor and keep avocados from turning brown.

Add remaining ingredients; mix well.

Serve with large corn tortilla chips, on a burger for a southwest-like flavor, mix 50-50 with your favorite salsa, or try it with chicken or fish dishes. Of course, you can simply eat it with a spoon...

Leftover guacamole can be stored in an airtight glass container. Press plastic wrap, wax paper, or parchment paper directly on the surface to keep it from turning brown. Refrigerate.

*Don't have fresh tomatoes on hand? Substitute 1 (14-ounce) can of organic, diced tomatoes - well drained.

Ham and Cheese Mini Biscuits

These fancy little biscuits with familiar ingredients are always a good idea.

1/2 cup butter, room temperature
1 1/2 cups grated sharp cheddar cheese
3/4 cup ham, finely diced
1 teaspoon Worcestershire sauce
1/2 teaspoon cayenne pepper
1 tablespoon Italian flat leaf parsley, finely chopped
1 cup all-purpose flour

Preheat oven to 350 degrees.

Combine butter and cheese in a medium-sized bowl; mix well. Add ham, Worcestershire sauce, cayenne pepper, and parsley; work all ingredients into the butter and cheese mixture to distribute evenly. Add the flour, a little at a time; mix well until well combined and a smooth ball of dough is formed.

Break off small pieces and roll in your hands to form small balls measuring about one-inch in diameter. Place balls on parchment-covered baking sheets; flatten slightly.

Bake 20-22 minutes until lightly browned.

Serve warm or at room temperature. If not used the same day they are made, these should be refrigerated in a covered container.

Mediterranean Olive Spread

Different and delectable, this layered dish is sure to please olive lovers everywhere. Beautiful.

3 tablespoons good olive oil, divided
1 cup sun-dried (or oven-dried) tomatoes in oil, drained and chopped
3 Roma tomatoes, seeded and chopped
4 cloves garlic, minced
1 red or orange bell pepper, seeded and chopped
1/2 cup water or broth
1/4 cup walnuts, chopped
1 slice hearty bread, torn in pieces
1/2 cup olive tapenade, homemade* or purchased
1 3/4 cup crumbled feta cheese, divided
3 6-inch flatbread (or pita) rounds, each cut in 8 wedges
1 teaspoon good olive oil

Preheat oven to 425 degrees. Use 1 tablespoon of the oil to coat the inside of a 1 1/2-quart shallow baking dish; set aside.

Heat the remaining oil in a large skillet. Add sun-dried tomatoes, Roma tomatoes, and garlic. Cook 4 minutes over medium heat. Add peppers; cook and stir an additional minute. Add water. Cover the skillet; simmer for 10 minutes. Stir in walnuts and bread pieces. Transfer cooked mixture to a food processor; pulse until smooth.

To finish, spoon half of the tomato mixture into the prepared baking dish and spread into an even layer. Distribute 3/4 cup of the cheese over the tomato layer.

Spread tapenade* (recipe, page 21) over the cheese, and smooth out in a thin layer. Spoon remaining tomato mixture over the tapenade, and spread evenly. Top with remaining cheese. Bake 20 minutes.

Reduce oven heat to 400 degrees. Brush flatbread or pita wedges with olive oil. Bake 5 minutes; flip the wedges over, and bake additional 5 minutes. Spoon olive spread on the warm wedges to serve.

The Nut Page

Spice up or sweeten up otherwise ordinary nuts for bowls full of goodness. Think about making an extra batch or two and sending some home with your guests.

Bourbon-Orange Pecans:

3 cups pecan halves
1/2 cup granulated sugar
1 tablespoon freshly grated orange peel
1/2 teaspoon kosher salt, and 1/2 teaspoon cayenne pepper
2 egg whites
3 tablespoons bourbon

Preheat oven to 300 degrees. Mix sugar, orange peel, salt, and cayenne. Beat egg whites until soft peaks form; add bourbon and beat well. Add sugar mixture and pecans; gently fold in until well coated. Transfer pecans to a rimmed baking sheet. Bake 30 minutes, stirring every 10 minutes. Pecans will crisp and separate. Remove from oven; break apart. Stir in an airtight container for up to one week.

Rosemary Walnuts:

2 cups walnuts (or pistachios)
2 1/2 tablespoons butter, melted
2 teaspoons dried rosemary, crushed
1/2 teaspoon kosher salt and 1/2 teaspoon cayenne pepper

Preheat oven to 350 degrees. Toss walnuts with butter, rosemary, salt, and cayenne. Transfer to a rimmed baking sheet. Bake 10 minutes. Cool.

Smoked Marcona Almonds:

2 cups Marcona almonds
1 tablespoon good olive oil
1 teaspoon smoked paprika
sea salt for finishing

Preheat oven to 350 degrees.
Mix almonds with oil and paprika. Transfer to a rimmed baking sheet. Bake 8-10 minutes. Sprinkle with salt while still warm.

COOKING WITH MORE CONFIDENCE

Oven Roasted Shrimp

4 servings

You will never boil shrimp again. Here is a foolproof way to prepare mouthwatering shrimp every time. Serve warm or chilled with your choice of these outstanding sauces.

1 pound large (16-20 count) raw shrimp, peeled and deveined
2 teaspoons freshly grated lemon peel
1 tablespoon fresh lemon juice
1 tablespoon good olive oil
1 teaspoon kosher salt
1 teaspoon freshly ground black pepper

Preheat oven to 400 degrees. Combine shrimp, lemon peel, juice, and olive oil in a bowl. Mix gently to coat all the shrimp evenly. Place shrimp on a rimmed baking sheet in one layer; sprinkle with salt and pepper. Roast for 6-7 minutes until the shrimp are firm, opaque, and pink in color. Remove from the oven, and serve with Thousand Island Dressing or Seafood Sauce.

Thousand Island Dressing:

A very versatile dressing - see Reuben Bites on Rye (recipe, page 30); great on sandwiches or salads.

1 cup mayonnaise
1 cup sour cream
2 tablespoons fresh lemon juice
3 tablespoons chili sauce
2 tablespoons onion, grated
2 tablespoons sweet pickle relish

1 1/2 tablespoons white wine vinegar
1 1/2 tablespoons ketchup
1 tablespoon dried dill weed
1/4 teaspoon kosher salt
1/2 teaspoon freshly ground black pepper

Combine mayonnaise and sour cream; mix until well blended. Add all remaining ingredients; stir well. Transfer to a glass container, cover tightly, and refrigerate until needed.

Seafood Sauce:

1/2 cup ketchup
1/2 cup chili sauce
1 teaspoon Worcestershire sauce
2 tablespoons lemon juice
1 tablespoon shallots, finely minced

1 tablespoon creamy horseradish
1/4 teaspoon onion powder
1/4 teaspoon hot sauce
1 teaspoon freshly ground black pepper

Mix all ingredients in a small bowl; cover tightly, and refrigerate until needed.

Parmesan Bread Dip

If you are looking for a special way to showcase local artisan breads, try this delightfully seasoned bread dip on your table.

1/4 pound Parmesan block cheese
1/4 pound Asiago block cheese
2 medium cloves garlic, minced
1 tablespoon green onion, finely chopped
1 teaspoon dried oregano
1/2 teaspoon red pepper flakes
1/2 teaspoon coarsely ground black pepper
3/4 cup good olive oil

Remove any existing rind from the cheeses; chop into small pieces. Place the cheese in a food processor; pulse until it forms a uniform, grainy texture. You will have about 2 cups in total.

Transfer the cheese to a bowl; stir in garlic and onion. Use a mortar and pestle (or your fingers) to break down the oregano releasing its fragrance and flavor; add along with all remaining ingredients. Stir well.

Place in a glass, covered container; let stand a few hours at room temperature to blend flavors before serving.

Reuben Bites on Rye

10 servings

A Reuben sandwich is one of my favorites to order at a great delicatessen. All of the familiar flavor is here in just a couple bites.

1 cup sauerkraut*, well drained and towel dried
3/4 pound cooked corned beef, finely chopped
2 teaspoons prepared horseradish
1/2 cup Thousand Island dressing (recipe, page 29)
1 1/2 cups shredded Gruyère (or other good quality Swiss cheese), divided
3 tablespoons cream cheese, room temperature
3/4 teaspoon caraway seeds, crushed
Rye crispy crackers
Dill pickle slices, chopped finely, for garnish

Chop the sauerkraut in small pieces. Place sauerkraut, corned beef, horseradish, and dressing in a medium saucepan; gently warm over very low heat. Add 3/4 cup Gruyère and cream cheese; stir in caraway seeds; mix well. Cover; cook over very low heat for 8-10 minutes, stirring occasionally.

Cool slightly; stir in remaining shredded cheese.

Serve on whole crackers for hearty bites, or cut each cracker in half for a mini version. Garnish with chopped pickles.

*I really preferred to use bagged sauerkraut found in the produce section (as opposed to using canned), as the flavor is fresher and brighter.

Smashed Potato Appetizer

6 servings

A simple potato has never tasted so good. Smashed, loaded, and baked. What's not to like.

3 medium Yukon Gold potatoes
1 tablespoon canola oil
2 tablespoons good olive oil
1/2 cup shredded cheddar cheese
1 tablespoon fresh parsley, finely chopped
3/4 teaspoon kosher salt
1/2 teaspoon coarsely ground black pepper
1/4 teaspoon cayenne pepper
1/2 cup sour cream
2 tablespoons green onions, very thinly sliced

Preheat oven to 400 degrees. Line a rimmed baking pan with foil; set aside.

Scrub potatoes; dry with a paper towel. Pierce each potato with a fork in several places. Coat the outside of each potato lightly with canola oil; place on prepared pan.

Bake 45-50 minutes, or until potatoes are fork-tender. Remove from oven; cool slightly.

Cut each potato in half; place (cut side down) on prepared pan. Smash them lightly with the bottom of a glass; drizzle with olive oil. Mix cheese, parsley, salt, black and cayenne peppers together; sprinkle evenly over smashed potatoes. Bake 20-25 minutes until potatoes are crispy and cheese has melted.

Transfer baked potatoes to a serving platter. Top with a small amount of sour cream; garnish with green onions.

Stuffed Mushrooms

Photograph, page 102   *8-10 servings*

Most starter tables include stuffed mushrooms; however, most don't taste like these. They are an exceptional balance of creamy, savory, and awesome. They will impress.

1 1/2 pounds (about 18) extra large white mushrooms
1/4 cup good olive oil
2 tablespoons brandy and 2 tablespoons dry white wine
2 tablespoons good olive oil
16 ounces uncooked, hot pork sausage
1/2 cup onions, minced
2 cloves garlic, minced
3 tablespoons dry sherry
3/4 teaspoon kosher salt and 1/2 teaspoon freshly ground black pepper
1 teaspoon fennel seed
1/2 cup fresh bread crumbs
8 ounces mascarpone cheese
3 tablespoons Asiago cheese, grated and 2 tablespoons Parmesan cheese, grated
1/4 cup fresh parsley, minced + 2 tablespoons extra for garnish

Preheat oven to 325 degrees.

Remove stems from mushrooms; trim ends. Using a melon baller or sharp spoon, remove gills and part of the flesh from inside mushrooms (making room to accept maximum stuffing). Finely chop mushroom stems and insides OR, as a timesaving shortcut, grind in a small food processor; set aside. Whisk oil, brandy, and wine together in a large bowl. Add mushroom caps; stir to coat completely, and set aside (this step assures another layer of flavor).

Heat 2 tablespoons oil in a large skillet over medium heat. Add sausage; cook and stir 8 minutes until crumbled and brown. Add onions; cook and stir 3 minutes. Add garlic, sherry, and reserved chopped mushroom stems; cook 1 more minute. Mix in salt, pepper, fennel, and bread crumbs. Add mascarpone; stir until creamy. Remove from heat; add Asiago and Parmesan cheeses and mix well. Cool mixture for 10 minutes. Fill each mushroom cap generously with stuffing. Place mushrooms in a shallow baking dish; garnish with parsley. Bake 45 minutes; the stuffing will be dark brown and toasted. Serve warm.

Triple Onion Bacon Dip

Give your vegetable platter a wake up call. It's addictive.

4 1/2 cups yellow onions (about 3 large), diced
1 tablespoon shallots, diced
1 1/2 tablespoons good olive oil
2 teaspoons kosher salt
1 teaspoon coarsely ground black pepper
1 teaspoon granulated sugar
1 tablespoon white wine vinegar
2 tablespoons dry white wine
6 slices bacon, diced
1 1/2 cups sour cream
1/4 cup plain Greek yogurt
1 tablespoon onion powder
1/8 teaspoon cayenne pepper
1/2 cup green onions, thinly sliced
celery, cucumbers, carrots, or other fresh vegetables of your choice

Preheat oven to 425 degrees. Line a large, rimmed baking pan with foil; set aside.
Thoroughly mix onions, shallots, oil, salt, pepper, and sugar; place on prepared pan in a single layer.
Roast in the oven for about 45 minutes, stirring every 10 minutes, until onions are soft and brown.
Remove from the oven; add vinegar and wine and stir well to combine. Return the onions to the oven, and
roast another 10 minutes. Cool. In a small skillet, cook bacon until crisp; cool. Add to the onion mixture.

To finish, combine sour cream, yogurt, onion powder, and cayenne pepper in a glass bowl. Stir in cooled
onion and bacon mixture. Add green onions; mix well. Serve with fresh vegetables.

This dip can be done up to 3 days ahead of time. Simply assemble as above without the green onions. Cover
tightly and refrigerate. Bring to room temperature and add onions before serving.

Warm Marinated Olives

Makes about 3 cups

My son, David, never met an olive he liked until he met these. This starter elevates regular olives to that gourmet level worthy of a special place on your table.

1/4 cup good olive oil
1/4 teaspoon cumin seeds
1/4 teaspoon anise seeds
8 black peppercorns
1 tablespoon freshly grated orange peel
1 teaspoon freshly grated lemon peel
2 cloves garlic, very thinly sliced
3 cups assorted (pitted) olives - such as: kalamata, manzanilla, black
2 tablespoons fresh orange juice
3-4 drops hot sauce
1 bay leaf

Heat oil in a skillet over medium heat. Add cumin, anise, peppercorns, orange and lemon peel, garlic and olives. Cook and stir over medium heat for 3 minutes until olives have warmed.

Remove skillet from heat; add orange juice, hot sauce, and bay leaf. Cool. Transfer to a glass bowl, cover tightly, and refrigerate several hours or overnight to blend flavors.

Just before serving, gently reheat olive mixture in a saucepan over low heat for 2-3 minutes until olives have warmed. Remove bay leaf and serve immediately.

Any leftovers may be covered, refrigerated, and reheated as needed.

Scoops of Confidence

For Starters

Starters are the first step on an evening's food journey. They should be special. Starters should also be:
> visually appealing (since we eat with our eyes first),
> cut small enough to be one bite if possible (certainly not larger unless you have a plate), and
> balanced in terms of flavors, food groups, hot and cold.

Have dishes and utensils for serving. Plan for these even if your party is potluck.

Give thought to including vegetarian and gluten-free options when planning a menu. Consider using a printed, informational card for each dish to give your guests a clue as to what it is, and what is in it.

Simply dialing back the portion size of a familiar entrée gives you a perfect appetizer.

Great emergency fill-ins? Extra cheeses, chips and salsa, nuts, French bread, or crackers. An already prepared roasted chicken from the deli will come in handy as well.

To prevent excess watery puddles on top of refrigerated sour cream or yogurt, smooth the surface with the back of a spoon, cover tightly, and refrigerate.

Think about doing food stations if you have minimal space. Different rooms, different food. Presenting desserts on a separate table gives them extra star power.

Setting up a buffet? Start with plates first, hot dishes next, cold dishes third. To minimize the juggling factor, reserve silverware and napkins for picking up last.

Have plenty of ice, and remember - guests will use more than one glass.

Good lighting and well chosen music help make the food journey memorable.

Gallus gallus domesticus

(rooster)

Breakfast, Brunches, Breads

Apple Bacon Egg Bake
Breakfast Frittata
Crunchy Granola
Eggs in the Oven
German Apple Pancake
Lemon Ricotta Pancakes
Morning Breakfast Cookies
Sweet and Savory Crepes
Sylvan Sunrise Breakfast
Waffles Two Ways
Wildwood's Wild Rice Quiche

Apricot Orange Bread
Blueberry Streusel Coffee Cake
Buttermilk Herb Biscuits
English Muffin Bread
Olive Bread
Raspberry Orange Muffins

Scoops of Confidence

Apple Bacon Egg Bake

6 servings

There is nothing more comforting than the aroma of baked apples and bacon in the morning.

8 slices crispy-fried bacon, crumbled
2 cups good eating apples (such as Honeycrisp), peeled, cored, and thinly sliced
1 1/2 tablespoons brown sugar
1/2 teaspoon cinnamon
1/4 teaspoon nutmeg
1 cup sharp cheddar or Gruyère cheese, shredded
3 eggs
1 cup half and half
1 cup all-purpose flour
1 1/2 teaspoons baking powder
1/4 teaspoon kosher salt

Preheat oven to 375 degrees. Coat a 9 x 9 x 2-inch baking dish with non-stick cooking spray; set aside.

Mix sliced apples with brown sugar, cinnamon, and nutmeg. Transfer to prepared dish; tap down to make one layer. Cover apples evenly with cheese. Distribute bacon crumbles on top.

In a medium bowl, beat eggs and cream. Add flour, baking powder, and salt; mix well. Spoon evenly over the apples, cheese, and bacon. Bake 30 minutes until lightly browned. Serve warm.

Breakfast Frittata

A breakfast frittata is an ideal centerpiece for a brunch. Add Raspberry Orange Muffins (recipe, page 55), fresh fruit, and hot coffee. You're all set.

3 tablespoons butter, divided
16 ounces ham, diced
1/2 cup onions, diced
1/4 cup celery, diced
1 large clove garlic, minced
2 tablespoons vegetable oil
4 cups fresh (not frozen), shredded hashbrowns
1 1/2 cups shredded Gruyère or Gouda cheese
6 eggs
1/2 cup cream or milk
1 cup fresh tomatoes, seeded and diced
1/4 teaspoon kosher salt
1/8 teaspoon freshly ground black pepper
1/8 teaspoon red pepper flakes

Preheat oven to 400 degrees.
Melt 1 tablespoon butter in a 10-inch ovenproof, non-stick skillet. Add ham, onions, and celery; cook 2-3 minutes until vegetables are tender. Add garlic; cook additional minute. Transfer mixture to a bowl. Reheat skillet; add 1 tablespoon butter and oil. Mix hashbrowns with salt and pepper; spoon into the skillet.

Using a spatula, pat potatoes into the bottom and up the sides of the skillet. (This will become your crust.) Brush the surface with remaining butter. Cook over medium heat until edges of the crust have started to turn golden brown. Remove pan from heat. Layer the cheese on top of the crust; spoon cooked ham mixture on top of the cheese. Beat eggs until frothy; stir in cream, tomatoes, salt, black and red pepper. Pour the egg mixture on top of cheese and ham. Bake 25-30 minutes. Test doneness by inserting a knife in the center; it should come out clean.

Remove from oven; let stand in the skillet for 5 minutes. Loosen edges, and transfer to a serving plate.

Crunchy Granola

Photograph, back cover and page 100   *Makes 10 cups*

This is not your typical seeds and sticks granola. Fresh and pure ingredients give you nutritious fuel to power your day a handful at a time.

1/3 cup light brown sugar, packed
1/3 cup pure maple syrup
1/2 cup canola oil
4 teaspoons pure vanilla extract
1/2 teaspoon kosher salt
1/2 teaspoon cinnamon
5 cups old-fashioned rolled oats
2 cups almonds (or walnuts), roughly chopped
2 cups raisins
1 cup dried, sweetened cranberries
1 cup dried apricots, roughly chopped

Preheat oven to 325 degrees. Line a large, rimmed baking sheet with parchment paper; coat lightly with non-stick cooking spray; set aside.

In a large bowl, whisk sugar and syrup until sugar is dissolved. Add oil, vanilla, salt, and cinnamon; stir until mixture is well blended. Add rolled oats and almonds; stir well.

Spoon mixture into the prepared pan. Bake 40-45 minutes until deep brown in color. Remove from oven; cool completely. Break into large chunks. Add raisins, cranberries, and apricots.

Store granola in an airtight container or zip top bag in your refrigerator.

You certainly could add whatever dried fruit you like to this recipe - think about apples or blueberries.

Eggs in the Oven

4-6 servings

An everyday answer to a hectic morning. It takes just as much time to put bread in the toaster as is does to put eggs in the oven. This will keep tummies satisfied until lunch.

8 eggs
1 cup sour cream
1 cup sharp cheddar cheese, shredded
1 tablespoon all-purpose flour
1/8 teaspoon bottled hot sauce
1/4 cup green onions, thinly sliced
2 tablespoons flat leaf parsley, minced
3/4 teaspoon kosher salt
1/2 teaspoon coarsely ground black pepper
1 1/2 tablespoons butter, melted

Preheat oven to 325 degrees. Coat a 2-quart shallow baking dish with non-stick cooking spray; set aside.

In a medium bowl, beat eggs until frothy. Add sour cream; mix well. Mix cheese with flour, stir into egg mixture. Add hot sauce, onions, parsley, salt, and pepper until well combined. Spoon into prepared dish. Drizzle melted butter over the top.

Bake 20-25 minutes until edges have browned and center is still a little jiggly. Remove from the oven.

Let rest for 5 minutes before serving, allowing eggs to set.

German Apple Pancake

6 servings

Honoring my heritage, this dish is an impressive alternative to regular pancakes and a great start to the day.

5 eggs
2 tablespoons granulated sugar
3/4 cup whole milk
1 teaspoon pure vanilla extract
3/4 cup all-purpose flour
1/2 teaspoon kosher salt
1/4 teaspoon freshly grated nutmeg
5 tablespoons butter
3 cups tart apples (such as Granny Smith) - peeled, cored, and thinly sliced
1 teaspoon fresh lemon juice
1/8 teaspoon kosher salt
2 tablespoons granulated sugar
2 teaspoons cinnamon
Topping:
1/4 cup confectioners' sugar for dusting on top
Sliced fresh strawberries and sweetened whipped cream for serving

Preheat oven to 425 degrees.

In a medium bowl, beat eggs and sugar. Add milk and vanilla; mix well. Whisk in flour, salt, and nutmeg to make a thin batter; set aside. Melt butter in a heavy 10-inch ovenproof skillet over medium heat. Add sliced apples, lemon juice, and salt; cook and stir 3 minutes until apples have softened. Add sugar and cinnamon; mix well. Using a spatula, pat down cooked apples evenly on the bottom of the skillet. Ladle pancake batter over apples. Immediately transfer skillet to the oven.

Bake 20 minutes. Pancake will be puffed and brown around the edges. The center will be set but still a bit jiggly. Sift confectioners' sugar evenly over the top. Transfer pancake to a large round serving platter; cut in wedges. Serve with berries and whipped cream.

Lemon Ricotta Pancakes

4 servings (8 pancakes)

Delicate and airy, these pancakes are pieces of breakfast heaven.

3 eggs, separated
3/4 cup ricotta cheese
1 tablespoon butter, softened
1/4 cup milk
1/3 cup all-purpose flour

2 teaspoons granulated sugar
1 1/2 teaspoons grated fresh lemon peel
1/4 teaspoon kosher salt
butter for the griddle and serving

Use 2 medium-sized, deep bowls. In the first bowl, beat egg whites until stiff peaks form; set aside. In the second bowl, beat egg yolks about 3 minutes until thick and pale yellow in color. Stir in ricotta, butter, and milk; mix well. Whisk flour, sugar, lemon peel, and salt together in another bowl; slowly stir in egg yolk and ricotta mixture, trying to keep batter light and airy. Gently fold in reserved, beaten egg whites.

Heat griddle to 375 degrees, or heat a non-stick skillet on medium. Melt just a little butter on the pan surface. Ladle 1/4 cup batter for each pancake onto the pan. Cook until bubbles cover the pancake surface; flip, and cook the other side until both the top and bottom are brown. Serve hot with butter and maple syrup or, to make them very special, Blueberry Sauce.

Blueberry Sauce:
2 cups blueberries, fresh or frozen
2/3 cup granulated sugar
1 cup orange juice
1/3 cup water
1/4 cup cold water mixed with 3 tablespoons cornstarch
1/2 teaspoon pure almond extract
1/2 teaspoon pure vanilla extract

Combine blueberries, sugar, orange juice and water in a medium saucepan. Cook and stir over low heat until sugar dissolves. Adjust heat to medium; bring to a boil. Reduce heat; stir in water and cornstarch mixture. Simmer 3 minutes. Remove from heat; stir in almond and vanilla extracts. Serve warm or at room temperature. This sauce is also terrific on ice cream.

Morning Breakfast Cookies

30 mini cookies

Cereal without the bowl. Stash in your pocket or a lunchbox.

1/4 cup butter, softened
1/3 cup honey
2 tablespoons milk or cream
1 teaspoon pure vanilla extract
1 ripe banana, mashed
1 cup flour
1 teaspoon cinnamon
1/2 teaspoon baking powder
1/4 teaspoon kosher salt
2 cups old fashioned rolled oats
1/2 cup walnuts, chopped
1/2 cup raisins or dried cherries, chopped

Preheat oven to 350 degrees. Coat mini muffin pans with non-stick cooking spray; set aside.

In a medium bowl, mix butter and honey until smooth and creamy. Add milk, vanilla, and banana; mix well. In a small bowl, whisk together flour, cinnamon, baking powder, and salt. Stir flour mixture into the butter mixture; mix well. Add oats, walnuts, and raisins; stir to combine.

Spoon enough batter into muffin cups to fill halfway. Bake 15 minutes until edges are brown and cookies feel solid when touched. Transfer to a wire rack to cool completely.

To use regular muffin tins for these cookies, preparation is the same. Just fill the cups 1/4 full.

Sweet and Savory Crepes

10 crepes

The batter is rich in eggs, giving the crepes their wonderful texture. Pair with either of these sweet or savory fillings.

Crepe Batter:

2 eggs	**1 tablespoon canola oil**
1 1/2 cups whole milk	**1/8 teaspoon kosher salt**
1 cup all-purpose flour	**2 tablespoons butter, melted**

Combine eggs, milk, flour, oil, and salt in a large bowl; beat on low speed until mixed. Beat on high speed a few seconds until smooth. Cover batter; chill at least 1 hour before using. Heat a 10-inch non-stick skillet 2-3 minutes over medium heat. Brush the inside of skillet with melted butter. Measure 1/4 cup batter, pour into one side of the skillet. Tilt the skillet and swirl batter to coat entire bottom. Cook about 1 minute until edges have started to brown and edges begin to curl. Loosen outside edges with a heatproof spatula; gently pick it up and flip it over. Cook additional 20-30 seconds. Transfer to a wire rack to cool.

Re-coat the pan with butter before cooking each crepe. Transfer crepe to a wire rack to cool. Once they have cooled, stack them between squares of parchment or waxed paper. Stored in a zip-top bag, they will keep in your refrigerator for several days or in your freezer for a month. All they require is a quick thaw, a reheat, and they're ready to use.

Sweet Peach:

Roll a few fresh peach slices in each crepe; transfer to a warm oven, along with additional slices in a separate dish. Make fresh peach sauce: In a medium saucepan over high heat, stir 2 cups crushed peaches, 1/2 cup granulated sugar, and 1/2 cup fresh orange juice until it comes to a boil. Reduce heat; simmer, uncovered for 15 minutes. Stir in 2 teaspoons fresh lemon juice and 1 teaspoon vanilla. To serve, put 2 peach-filled crepes on each plate. Top with reserved peach slices and warm peach sauce.

Savory Chicken and Mushroom:

Preheat oven to 400 degrees. Heat 1 tablespoon canola oil and 1 tablespoon butter over medium-high heat until very hot. add 8 ounces sliced mushrooms, 1/2 teaspoon kosher salt, and 1/8 teaspoon black pepper. Cook and stir 7-8 minutes. Transfer to a bowl; set aside. Add 1 tablespoon butter to the skillet with 1 cup diced orange bell pepper, 1 teaspoon chopped fresh rosemary, and 1/4 teaspoon kosher salt; cook 8 minutes on medium heat. Stir in 1 tablespoon flour, 2 cups diced cooked chicken (recipe, page 68), 1 1/2 cups diced tomatoes, 1 cup chicken broth, and 1/2 teaspoon red pepper flakes; cook and stir 4 minutes. Stir in reserved mushrooms. Fill crepe with 3 tablespoons filling; place in buttered baking dish, and top with Parmesan cheese. Bake 15 minutes.

Sylvan Sunrise Breakfast

4 servings

This was created for my son David's breakfast early one morning at the lake. It is my simple answer to a skillet scramble.

4 ounces hot pork sausage
3 tablespoons butter
2 cups fresh, shredded hashbrowns
1/2 teaspoon kosher salt, divided
1/2 teaspoon freshly ground black pepper, divided
3 eggs
3 tablespoons heavy cream
1 cup shredded mozzarella cheese
2 tablespoons fresh parsley, minced
Fresh fruit of your choice for serving

In a 9-inch non-stick skillet, break up sausage into small crumbles. Cook and stir over medium heat until sausage has browned; transfer to a small plate. In the same skillet over low heat, melt butter and scrape up any flavorful brown bits in the bottom of the pan. Add hashbrowns, 1/4 teaspoon salt, and 1/4 teaspoon pepper; toss with a fork to mix well. Press hashbrowns evenly on the bottom and halfway up the sides of the skillet.

Whisk eggs, cream, 1/4 teaspoon salt, and 1/4 teaspoon pepper together in a medium bowl. Stir in cheese and reserved sausage; mix well. Spoon evenly over hashbrowns in the skillet. Sprinkle the top with parsley. Adjust heat to medium. Cook 3 minutes - using a fork, wiggle the liquid down and around so filling can cook evenly. (You may have to tip the pan a little so the liquid levels out.) Reduce heat to medium low.

Cover the skillet; cook 8-10 minutes until hashbrowns are brown and crispy at the edges of the pan and the eggs look fairly dry and cooked.

Turn off heat. Keep the skillet covered, and allow to rest 5 minutes. Cut in wedges to serve.

Waffles Two Ways

Who doesn't like waffles? Here are two tried and true versions that are sure to please.

Buttermilk Waffles:

3 eggs, separated
2 tablespoons granulated sugar
1 1/2 cups buttermilk
2/3 cup whole milk
1/3 cup butter, melted and cooled to room temperature

2 1/4 cups all-purpose flour
2 teaspoons baking powder
1 teaspoon baking soda
3/4 teaspoon kosher salt

Preheat oven to 250 degrees. Place a wire cooling rack in the middle section of your oven - this will be used to keep waffles warm. Preheat waffle iron according to manufacturer's instructions.

For the waffles, beat egg whites in a small, deep bowl until soft peaks form. Add sugar; beat until stiff peaks form. In another bowl, mix egg yolks, buttermilk, milk, and melted butter. Add flour, baking powder, soda, and salt; mix well. Fold in egg white mixture. Your batter should be thick and airy. Each should use about 1/2 cup batter, but check your waffle iron's instructions to make sure. Transfer to the warmed oven (in a single layer) to keep them crisp. Serve with toppings of your choice.

Banana Oatmeal Waffles :

8 servings

1 cup old fashioned rolled oats
1 cup all-purpose flour
3 tablespoons brown sugar, packed
1 tablespoon baking powder
1/2 teaspoon baking soda
1/4 cup butter, melted and cooled to room temperature

1/2 teaspoon ground cinnamon
1/8 teaspoon ground nutmeg
1 1/2 cups buttermilk
2 eggs, beaten
2 medium bananas, peeled and diced

In a medium bowl, combine oats, flour, sugar, baking powder, soda, cinnamon, and nutmeg; set aside. In another bowl, mix buttermilk and eggs until well blended; stir in bananas and butter. Add flour mixture; gently stir to blend.

Make waffles according to your waffle iron's instructions. Transfer to a warmed oven. Serve with sliced bananas and warm maple syrup.

Wildwood's Wild Rice Quiche

Photograph, page 101   *6 servings*

Wildwood, located next to Maplewood State Park here in Minnesota, is one of our family's happy places. Whenever you sit down for brunch at Bob and Karen's, this dish is certain to be on the table.

1 9-inch piecrust*
1 tablespoon butter
8 ounces hot pork sausage
1/2 cup green onions, thinly sliced
3 eggs
1 1/2 cups half and half
1/2 teaspoon kosher salt
1/4 teaspoon freshly ground black pepper
1/4 teaspoon bottled hot sauce
1 cup cheddar cheese, grated
1 teaspoon finely chopped, fresh parsley
1 1/4 cups cooked wild rice

Preheat oven to 400 degrees.

Place pie crust in a glass pie plate; fold edges and crimp; set aside.

Melt butter over medium heat in a skillet. Add sausage; break up into crumbles with a fork, and cook until well browned. Stir in onions; set aside. In another bowl, beat eggs. Add cream, salt, pepper, and hot sauce; set aside. Mix cheese and parsley together; set aside.

To assemble, scatter half the sausage and onion mixture into prepared crust. Distribute half the wild rice and half the cheese mixture evenly over the sausage layer. Repeat with remaining sausage and wild rice. Carefully spoon egg mixture over the layers. Top with remaining cheese and parsley. Bake 15 minutes. Reduce oven temperature to 350 degrees; bake additional 30 minutes until the filling feels set to the touch - should not jiggle when you move it. Cool on a rack at least 30 minutes before slicing and serving. If made ahead, cover with plastic wrap and refrigerate. When ready to serve, bring to room temperature. Cut in wedges; reheat in a 350 degree oven 20-25 minutes until thoroughly warmed.

*Pie Pastry (recipe, page 56)

Apricot Orange Bread

Makes 1 loaf

Apricots and cranberries add unexpected bursts of flavor in this sweet bread.

1 cup granulated sugar
1 egg
2 tablespoons vegetable oil
2 tablespoons frozen orange juice concentrate, thawed
1 tablespoon freshly grated orange peel
1/3 cup orange juice
1/3 cup whole milk
3/4 cup dried apricots, diced
2/3 cup dried cranberries
2 1/4 cups all purpose flour
2 teaspoons baking powder
1/2 teaspoon baking soda
1/4 teaspoon kosher salt
1 1/2 teaspoons sanding or coarse sugar for topping.

Preheat oven to 350 degrees. Grease and flour a 9 x 5 x 3-inch loaf pan; set aside.

In a large bowl, combine sugar, egg, and oil; mix until thick and creamy. Stir in orange juice concentrate, peel, juice, and milk. Add apricots and cranberries.

In a separate bowl, whisk flour, baking powder, soda, and salt together. Gently fold flour mixture into the egg mixture until no traces of flour remain. Spoon batter into prepared pan. Sprinkle with sugar.

Bake 60 minutes until toothpick inserted in the center of the loaf comes out clean, and sides pull slightly away from the edges of the pan.

Cool thoroughly on a wire rack before slicing to serve.

Blueberry Streusel Coffee Cake

12 servings

How about a morning treat using some of those plump summer blueberries? What a great excuse to invite the neighbors over for coffee.

1/2 cup butter, softened
3/4 cup brown sugar, packed
1/2 cup granulated sugar
2 eggs
1/2 cup buttermilk
1/4 cup plain yogurt
1 3/4 cup all-purpose flour
3/4 teaspoon baking powder
1/2 teaspoon baking soda
1/2 teaspoon kosher salt
2 teaspoons freshly grated lemon peel
1 1/2 cups blueberries*, mixed with 2 teaspoons all-purpose flour

Streusel:
4 tablespoons butter
1/3 cup brown sugar
1/3 cup all-purpose flour
3/4 teaspoon ground cinnamon
1/4 teaspoon kosher salt
2/3 cup pecans, finely chopped

Frosting Drizzle:
1 cup confectioners' sugar
3 tablespoons milk or cream
1/2 teaspoon pure vanilla extract

Preheat oven to 350 degrees. Coat a 9-inch round or square pan with non-stick cooking spray; set aside. In a medium bowl, cream butter and sugars until light and fluffy. Add eggs, one at a time, beating after each addition. Stir in buttermilk and yogurt; mix well. Whisk flour, baking powder, soda, and salt together in a separate bowl; stir into egg mixture. Combine all streusel ingredients. To assemble, spoon half of batter evenly into prepared pan. Distribute half of the blueberries on top. Sprinkle with half of the streusel topping. Repeat layers with remaining batter, blueberries, and streusel topping. Bake 45 minutes until toothpick inserted in the center comes out clean. Cool. Combine frosting ingredients; mix well. Drizzle over the cooled cake; cut in squares to serve.

* Fresh or frozen blueberries can be used.

Buttermilk Herb Biscuits

Bring back the biscuits. This recipe is reminiscent of those we used to make at home on the farm almost daily. I like to pair them with my hearty Italian Meatball Soup (recipe, page 63).

2 cups all-purpose flour
1 tablespoon baking powder
1 teaspoon granulated sugar
1/4 teaspoon kosher salt
1/4 teaspoon freshly ground black pepper
1 teaspoon dried dill weed
1 tablespoon fresh parsley, finely chopped
3/4 cup buttermilk
1/4 cup canola oil
1 tablespoon melted butter
1/4 teaspoon freshly ground black pepper for topping

Preheat oven to 425 degrees.

In a medium bowl, whisk together flour, baking powder, sugar, salt, pepper, dill weed, and parsley.
In another bowl, whisk buttermilk and oil together; add to the flour mixture. Mix with a fork until blended.

Bring dough together with your hands, and turn it out onto a lightly floured board. Pat dough out to a 3/4-inch thickness. Using a 2-inch biscuit cutter, cut into rounds. Transfer biscuits to a baking sheet. Brush the top of each biscuit with melted butter and a tiny sprinkle of black pepper.

Bake about 15 minutes until puffed and golden. Cool slightly before serving.

English Muffin Bread

Toast perfection, with lots of nooks and crannies for butter and jam.

1/4 cup cornmeal for dusting the pans
5 cups bread flour
1 1/2 tablespoons instant yeast
1 tablespoon granulated sugar
2 1/2 teaspoons kosher salt
1 teaspoon baking soda
3 cups whole milk, warmed to 120 degrees

Generously coat two 8 1/2 x 4 1/2-inch loaf pans (glass or metal) with shortening. Dust insides with cornmeal; shake out excess, and set aside.

Whisk flour, yeast, sugar, salt, and baking soda together in a large bowl. Stir warmed milk (use an instant read thermometer to test exact 120 degree temperature - milk will interact immediately with the yeast) into the flour mixture to form a sticky, thick batter.

Coat a sheet of plastic wrap with non-stick cooking spray; place over the bowl. Allow to rise 30 minutes in a warm place. (At this point, it will look bubbly and will have doubled in volume.) Give the dough a stir to deflate. Divide evenly between two prepared pans. Once again, cover the pans with sprayed plastic wrap. Let rise another 30 minutes, at which time dough will have reached the top of each pan.

Heat oven to 375 degrees.

Remove plastic wrap from each loaf. Bake 30 minutes until bread has browned. Take its temperature to be sure of doneness. It should register 200 degrees.

Transfer loaves to a wire rack for about an hour to cool completely. Slice, toast, and serve.

Olive Bread

One free-form loaf

Afraid to make bread from scratch? Try this easy step-by-step recipe to make a beautiful loaf of bread with great taste and texture. Ridiculously good toasted with a thin slice of Gruyère.

2 1/2 to 3 cups bread flour, divided
1 package (2 1/4 teaspoons) instant yeast
2 tablespoons granulated sugar
1 teaspoon kosher salt
1/3 cup hot water (125 degrees)
2 large eggs
1/4 cup butter, softened
1 cup ripe olives, pitted and well drained
1 cup green pimiento-stuffed olives, well drained
1 egg yolk, beaten
cornmeal for preparing baking pan
1/2 teaspoon extra coarse sea salt

Sprinkle cornmeal on a large 16-inch baking sheet; set aside. Place 2 cups of the flour, yeast, sugar, and salt into a medium-sized work bowl. Using a whisk or fork, stir well to blend. Make a well in the center of the flour mixture. Add hot water; stir to form a batter. Add eggs; stir vigorously. Add butter in small pieces. Use a wooden spoon (or with a stand mixer, a flat blade) to stir until batter is silky smooth. Add remaining flour, a little at a time, until dough forms a ball and is not sticky to the touch. Knead by hand on a floured surface (or in a stand mixer, using the dough hook) about 6-8 minutes. Dough should be smooth and elastic. Place dough in a large, well-greased bowl; cover with plastic wrap, and set in a warm place to rise until doubled in size (about 45-60 minutes).

Preheat oven to 350 degrees. Punch the dough down and turn onto a floured surface. Pat the dough into a 14-inch square; let it rest for five minutes to allow the dough to relax. Mix the olives together and scatter evenly onto the dough; press lightly into place. Gently roll up, jellyroll fashion, pinching the seam together and tucking under ends. Flatten the roll slightly to form and shape an oval about 2 inches thick. Transfer the loaf to prepared pan, seam side down. Cover with plastic wrap; let rest for about 20 minutes to rise again. It will look puffy. Remove plastic wrap. Use a pastry brush to coat entire surface with beaten egg yolk. Sprinkle with sea salt. Bake 40-45 minutes until loaf is nicely browned. Cool slightly. Slice thinly; serve warm or at room temperature. To reheat, place in a 325 degree oven for 15-20 minutes.

Raspberry Orange Muffins

16 muffins

Raspberries are one of my favorite seasonal fruits. Coupled with a fresh burst of orange flavor, these muffins are scrumptious.

1/2 cup butter, softened
1 cup granulated sugar
2 eggs, room temperature
1 1/2 tablespoons frozen orange juice concentrate, thawed
1 teaspoon pure vanilla extract
1 1/2 tablespoons freshly grated orange peel
3 cups all-purpose flour
1 tablespoon baking powder
1/2 teaspoon baking soda
1 teaspoon kosher salt
1 1/2 cups plain yogurt
2 cups fresh raspberries
1/3 cup sanding (coarse) sugar* for topping

Preheat oven to 375 degrees. Coat muffin pans with non-stick cooking spray; set aside.

In a medium bowl, combine butter and sugar; beat until light and fluffy. Add eggs, one at a time, beating after each addition. Stir in orange juice concentrate, vanilla, and orange peel. In a separate bowl, whisk together flour, baking powder, soda, and salt. Add about half of the dry ingredients to the egg mixture; mix well. Gently stir in about half of the yogurt. Stir remaining dry ingredients. Finish with remaining yogurt; stir just to barely blend ingredients. (Your batter will be very thick.)

Spoon a generous tablespoon of batter into each muffin cup. Press 2 raspberries, top-side down, into the batter. Fill each cup almost to the top. Press 1 or 2 more raspberries, top-side up, into each muffin; sprinkle generously with sugar. Bake 20 minutes until tops are golden, and a toothpick inserted in the center comes out clean. Cool on a wire rack.

*Coarse sugar adds a pretty dose of "bling" to overall appearance. Substitute granulated sugar if you don't have this ingredient in your pantry.

Scoops of Confidence

For Breakfast, Brunches, and Breads

Accurate measuring is very important. Use both dry and liquid measuring cups. They are not interchangeable. To accurately measure flour, for instance, spoon it into a dry measuring cup and level with a straight edged spatula. Dry measuring cups should also be used for semisolids such as peanut butter, mayonnaise and sour cream. To use liquid measuring cups, pour in liquid and read measurement at eye level.

Make sure you check expiration dates on yeast, baking powder and baking soda. They are far less effective if out-of-date. The fresher, the better.

When making biscuits, flour your biscuit cutter and cut straight down through the dough. Do not twist the cutter - this would crimp the edges, and your biscuits won't raise as well when baked.

Too many ripe bananas? Mash them inside a zip top freezer bag, and pop in the freezer. To thaw, place the bag of frozen bananas in warm water - they will be ready to use in your muffins or breads in just a few minutes.

To crumble cheese in your food processor, cut it into small chunks first. Add a little cornstarch or flour to prevent clumping, and results in an easier melting cheese (Use ratio 1/4 teaspoon for every 1 cup cheese.)

Oven Roasted Bacon:

Preheat oven to 400 degrees, with rack in the middle position. Line a heavy, rimmed baking pan with foil. Arrange bacon slices in one layer to fit. Bake 7 minutes. Rotate pan front to back; bake additional 7 minutes. Remove from oven; blot excess fat from bacon with paper towels. Cool used pan, and discard foil.

Pie Pastry (makes 1 9-inch deep dish crust):

1 1/4 cups all-purpose flour   **1/4 cup vegetable shortening**
1/2 teaspoon kosher salt   **5 tablespoons ice water**
1 teaspoon granulated sugar
1/4 cup butter, chilled, cut in small pieces

Whisk flour, salt, and sugar together. Using a pastry blender, cut in butter and shortening until mixture resembles coarse crumbs. Sprinkle with water; toss quickly with a fork until most particles stick together (do not overmix). Gather the pastry and form into a flat disk; cover with plastic wrap, and chill 30 minutes. Preheat oven to 375 degrees. Roll out to a 14-inch circle on a lightly floured surface. Place pastry in a glass pie plate; fold over edges and crimp in place. Should you be needing a pre baked crust, use a fork to pierce the sides and bottom (to allow steam escape during baking). Bake 25 minutes or until crust is light brown in color.

Lactuca sativa

(romaine lettuce)

Soups and Salads

Broth 101
Butternut Squash Bisque
Cream of Broccoli Soup
Gingered Chicken Soup
Italian Meatball Soup
Potato Bacon Chowder
Smokey Shrimp Chowder
Tomato Soup with Cheese Croutons
Beef Vegetable Stew
White Chicken Chili

Asian Pear Salad
Cashew Chicken Salad
Cauliflower Almond Salad
Cucumber Radish Salad
Emma's Summer Salad
Farro Vegetable Salad
Fresh and Frozen Fruit Salad
Fresh Asparagus Salad
Italian Pasta Salad
Lemon Drop Salad
Roasted Pear Salad

Scoops of Confidence

Broth 101

Easy to make and very flavorful. Two versions of basic homemade broth that will become staples and save you a trip to the store. Both can be refrigerated up to three days, or frozen up to three months. Neither recipe contains salt, so you will want to double check the seasonings in any soup or dish you make with the broth.

Vegetable Broth:
2 large onions, unpeeled and quartered
3 leeks (white and light green part only) - halved, washed, cut in 2-inch pieces
3 medium carrots, peeled and cut in 2-inch pieces
3 medium tomatoes, coarsely chopped
2 cloves garlic, peeled
2 tablespoons good olive oil
1 large celery stalk and leaves, cut in 2-inch pieces
2 bay leaves
6 peppercorns

Preheat oven to 450 degrees. Place onions, leeks, carrots, tomatoes, and garlic in a large roasting pan. Toss with oil. Roast 15 minutes; stir, and roast additional 15 minutes. Transfer vegetables and any browned bits from the pan to a large stockpot. Add celery, bay leaves, and peppercorns. Add 8 cups cold water. Bring to a boil; reduce heat, and simmer for 45 minutes. Do not stir. Line a colander or strainer (set over a large heatproof bowl) with a paper towel or double layer of cheesecloth. Strain stock. Discard cooked vegetables. Transfer cooled broth to a glass container, cover tightly, and refrigerate. Remove all chilled fat from the broth before using.

Chicken or Turkey Broth:
2 skeletons (left from rotisserie or roasted birds), or about 3 pounds bone-in parts (use both breasts and thighs for best flavor), uncooked
Use the same ingredients - minus leeks, tomatoes, and oil - from the recipe for Vegetable Broth.

Put the vegetables and chicken or turkey parts in a large stockpot. Add cold water to cover meat and vegetables by 1 inch. Bring to a boil, reduce heat, and simmer for 3-4 hours. Skim fat from surface every 45 minutes or so. Do not stir. Add cold water periodically to keep the vegetables and meat totally covered at all times. Strain stock; discard bones, vegetables, and meat. Transfer cooled broth to a glass container, cover tightly, and refrigerate. Remove all chilled fat from the broth before using.

Butternut Squash Bisque

All of your favorite flavors of fall come together in one bowl. Comfort at its best.

3 1/2 cups fresh butternut squash (about 3 pounds), roasted
3 tablespoons butter
1 1/2 cups yellow onions, diced
1 1/2 cups celery, diced
1 1/2 cups tart apples (such as Granny Smith), diced
1 large clove garlic, minced
3 cups chicken broth*
1 teaspoon kosher salt
1 teaspoon curry
1/2 teaspoon cinnamon
1/4 teaspoon nutmeg
1/2 cup light cream
1/2 teaspoon freshly ground black pepper
1/4 cup chives, snipped in small pieces

Preheat oven to 425 degrees. Line a rimmed baking sheet with parchment (or foil). Coat the surface lightly with pan spray or oil; set aside.

For ease of cutting the whole squash, microwave for 1 minute on high power. Cool slightly to handle it safely; cut in half lengthwise. Remove seeds. Place the halves (cut side down) on prepared baking sheet. Roast 35-40 minutes until the squash is very tender. Remove from oven; set aside to cool slightly.

Heat butter in a 2-quart, heavy saucepan. Add onions, celery, and apples; cook and stir over medium heat for 10 minutes. Reduce heat to low. Add garlic, roasted squash, chicken both, salt, curry, cinnamon, and nutmeg. Simmer 15 minutes. Transfer soup to a blender** (or use an immersion blender right in the cooking pot); puree until smooth. Return soup to the pot to reheat; stir in cream. Ladle soup into individual bowls. Sprinkle each serving lightly with pepper; garnish with chives.

*Chicken Broth (recipe, page 59)
**Warm soup expands quickly in a blender - make sure this step is done in small batches.

Cream of Broccoli Soup

An amazing bowl of soup awaits. Broccoli and bacon are wonderful partners.

8 slices bacon, diced
1 1/2 pounds broccoli
2 tablespoons butter
1 cup onions, diced
3/4 cup celery, diced
1/3 cup all-purpose flour
3 cloves garlic, minced
1/4 cup dry white wine
1 cup chicken broth*
3 cups vegetable broth*
1 bay leaf
1/2 cup heavy cream
1 teaspoon kosher salt
1/2 teaspoon freshly ground black pepper

In a medium skillet, fry bacon pieces until crisp. Transfer cooked bacon to a paper towel to drain; set aside. To prepare broccoli, cut small florets from the stems. Peel stems, slice thinly; set aside.

Discard all but 2 tablespoons of the bacon fat in the skillet. Add onions, celery, and sliced broccoli stems; cook and stir 6 minutes until vegetables are tender. Stir in flour and garlic; cook and stir 1 minute. Whisk in wine and chicken broth.

In a large saucepan, bring the vegetable broth and bay leaf to a boil. Add broccoli florets; cook about 3 minutes until crisp-tender. Remove florets from the broth with a slotted spoon; set aside. Discard bay leaf. Add cooked vegetable mixture to the warm broth; cook 5 minutes on medium low heat, Stir in cream, salt, pepper, and half the reserved broccoli florets. Simmer additional 5 minutes. Puree soup with an immersion blender in the saucepan, or in a regular blender. Take extra time for this step to make sure soup is as smooth as possible. Return warm soup to the saucepan; add reserved florets and gently simmer 2 minutes. To serve, ladle hot soup into individual bowls. Garnish with reserved bacon pieces.

*Chicken and Vegetable Broth (recipes, page 59)

Gingered Chicken Soup

10 generous servings

Fresh ginger takes chicken soup in a surprisingly different and healthy direction. If you're looking for a gluten-free option, this one is a beauty.

2 tablespoons good olive oil
1 1/2 cups onions, diced
2 cups celery, diced
4 cloves garlic, minced
3 tablespoons fresh ginger, peeled and grated
8 cups chicken broth*
3 cups cooked and shredded boneless, skinless chicken breasts
2 1/2 cups carrots, sliced
1 tablespoon apple cider vinegar
1 teaspoon kosher salt
1/2 teaspoon freshly ground black pepper
1/4 teaspoon ground turmeric
2 cups fresh mushrooms, thinly sliced
1 1/2 cups fresh or frozen peas
1/4 cup fresh parsley, minced
1/2 cup green onions, thinly sliced for garnish

Heat olive oil in a 4 1/2-quart soup pot or saucepan. Add onions and celery; cook and stir over medium heat for 5-6 minutes. Add garlic and ginger; cook and stir for 2 minutes. Stir in broth, chicken, carrots, and vinegar; cook 10-12 minutes until carrots are crisp-tender. Add salt, pepper, turmeric, and mushrooms; cook additional 10 minutes. Stir in peas and parsley; simmer 3 minutes.

To serve, ladle into individual bowls; garnish each serving with a few green onions.

*Chicken Broth (recipe, page 59)

Refrigerate any extra soup in a covered glass container up to 3 days.

Italian Meatball Soup

Have a Italian experience with this outstanding soup. It's so well seasoned and just right for a meal on its own.

Meatballs:
1/2 pound ground beef
1/2 pound ground pork
1 egg, slightly beaten
1/4 cup fresh parsley, minced
2 large cloves garlic, minced
3/4 teaspoon kosher salt
1/2 teaspoon black pepper
1/2 teaspoon dried oregano
1/2 teaspoon onion powder
1/2 teaspoon Hungarian paprika
1/4 teaspoon dried thyme
1/8 teaspoon cayenne pepper
1/2 cup grated Parmesan cheese

Soup:
2 tablespoons good olive oil
3/4 cup onions, diced
2/3 cup celery, diced
2/3 cup carrots, diced
2 tablespoons tomato paste
1 cup russet potatoes, diced
1 14-ounce can diced tomatoes
4 cups beef broth
1 teaspoon dried oregano
3/4 teaspoon kosher salt
1/2 teaspoon black pepper
1 cup shaved Parmesan cheese

Combine beef and pork; add egg, and mix thoroughly. Gently mix in remaining ingredients until well combined. Roll into tiny 1-inch meatballs. In a 4 1/2-quart soup pot or saucepan, heat olive oil over medium heat. Add meatballs and cook about 4 minutes, stirring occasionally, until browned on all sides. Do not crowd - you may have to brown these in two batches. Transfer meatballs to a plate with a slotted spoon; set aside.

To make the soup, add onions, celery, and carrots to remaining oil in the cooking pot; cook and stir about 3-4 minutes until vegetables are tender. Add tomato paste and potatoes; cook additional 2 minutes. Stir in tomatoes, beef broth, and reserved meatballs; bring to a boil. Reduce heat; add oregano, salt, and pepper. Simmer 15 minutes.

To serve, ladle soup into individual bowls; top with shaved Parmesan cheese.

Potato Bacon Chowder

Photograph, page 110   *6 servings*

For sure, you will want to have more than one bowl. Guests will like it so much they will want to do the dishes.

8 slices bacon, cut in 1/4-inch slices
2 tablespoons butter
3/4 cup onions, diced
1/2 cup celery, diced
3 cloves fresh garlic, minced
1/4 cup all-purpose flour
4 cups chicken broth*
1/2 cup half and half
2 1/2 cups russet potatoes, diced (about 2 large)
2 cups fresh or frozen corn kernels
1/2 cup sour cream
3/4 teaspoon kosher salt
3/4 teaspoon freshly ground black pepper
1/2 teaspoon bottled hot sauce
1/4 cup green onions, thinly sliced

In a large Dutch oven or heavy cooking pot, cook and stir bacon pieces until brown and crispy; transfer to a paper towel lined plate to drain. Pour out all bacon drippings. Add 2 tablespoons drippings back to the pot along with the butter. Add celery and onions; cook and stir for 3 minutes over medium heat until they are opaque and tender. Add garlic; cook and stir 1 minute. Mix in flour with a fork; scrape up all brown bits from the pan. Whisk in broth and cream. Add potatoes; cook about 8 minutes on medium heat until they are tender. Add corn, sour cream, salt, pepper, and hot sauce. Simmer 10 minutes. Stir in onions and about 3/4 of reserved bacon. Ladle soup into individual bowls, topping each with a few pieces of bacon.

*Chicken Broth (recipe, page 59)

This soup can be refrigerated in a tightly covered glass container for up to 3 days. Because cream in the soup will break down and compromise texture, I would not recommend freezing.

COOKING WITH MORE CONFIDENCE

Smokey Shrimp Chowder

6 generous servings

This may be served alone as a soup, or consider serving it over cooked rice for a satisfying main dish. Smoked paprika adds a rich intensity of flavor.

4 slices bacon, diced
1 pound large (26-30 count) shrimp, peeled and deveined
1 tablespoon butter
1 cup onions, diced
1 cup celery, diced
1 1/2 cups red potatoes, peeled and diced
3 large cloves garlic, minced
2 teaspoons smoked paprika
1 1/2 teaspoons dried oregano
1/2 teaspoon dried basil
1/4 teaspoon red pepper flakes
3/4 teaspoon kosher salt
1/2 teaspoon freshly ground black pepper
4 cups chicken broth*
1 bay leaf
1/2 cup heavy cream
2 cups corn kernels, fresh (or, if frozen, thawed)
1 tablespoon fresh parsley, minced

Fry bacon in a large, deep pot until crispy. Remove bacon from pan; drain on paper towels. Reserve about 2 tablespoons drippings in pan; add shrimp and cook 2-3 minutes until pink in color. Remove shrimp from pan and set aside. Add butter, onions, celery, and potatoes to the pan. Cook and stir about 5-6 minutes until vegetables are tender. Add garlic; cook 1 minute. Season with paprika, oregano, basil, red pepper, salt, and pepper. Whisk in broth; add bay leaf. Bring to a boil, reduce heat, and simmer 12 minutes until slightly thickened. Discard bay leaf. Stir in cream.

At this point, chowder may be pureed with an immersion blender in the cooking pot, or in two batches using a regular blender. Return pureed chowder to the cooking pot. Add shrimp, corn, parsley, and reserved bacon. Gently re-warm chowder over very low heat before serving.

*Chicken Broth (recipe, page 59)

Tomato Soup and Cheese Croutons

Real homemade taste and texture. A shortcut to the classic combination of soup and grilled cheese.

Soup:

1 tablespoon butter
1 teaspoon good olive oil
1 1/4 cups onions, diced
1 cup celery, diced
3 cloves fresh garlic, minced
2 28-ounce cans whole tomatoes; undrained
1 cup water
1 tablespoon granulated sugar
2 teaspoons kosher salt
1/2 teaspoon freshly ground black pepper
1/4 teaspoon red pepper flakes
1/4 teaspoon celery seed
1/4 teaspoon dried oregano
2/3 cup heavy cream

Croutons:

4 slices rustic bread
3 tablespoons butter
1/2 cup grated cheddar cheese

Make croutons first. Preheat oven to 350 degrees. Cut bread into 4-inch chunks, discarding crusts, then into 3/4-inch cubes. Melt butter in an ovenproof skillet; stir until butter is brown. Add bread cubes; toss to coat evenly. Transfer skillet to the oven; bake about 15 minutes until croutons are golden brown, stirring occasionally. Remove from oven; turn off the heat. Sprinkle croutons with cheese. Just before serving, return skillet to the warm (but not hot) oven 2-3 minutes to re-warm.

In a large saucepan or soup pot, heat butter and oil. Add onions and celery; cook and stir 5 minutes. Add garlic; cook 1 more minute. Add tomatoes and water; cook 10 minutes over medium heat. Stir in sugar, salt, black and red pepper, celery seed, and oregano. Simmer 10 minutes. Remove from heat; stir in cream. Puree with an immersion blender right in the soup pot, or process in a blender in two batches.

Gently reheat soup over very low heat. Ladle soup into individual bowls and top with warm croutons.

Beef Vegetable Stew

8 generous servings

Make the Buttermilk Herb Biscuits (recipe, page 52) and serve them with this classic stew, so rich in hearty beef goodness.

3 pounds beef chuck roast, cut in 1 1/2-inch pieces
2 teaspoons kosher salt
1 teaspoon freshly ground black pepper
2 tablespoons vegetable oil, 1 tablespoon butter
2 cups onions, diced
6 cloves fresh garlic, minced
1 1/2 tablespoons tomato paste
2 cups carrots, peeled and sliced in 3/4-inch pieces
2 cups celery, cut in 3/4-inch pieces
2 cups red wine
4 cups beef broth
2 tablespoons balsamic vinegar
1 tablespoon Worcestershire sauce
1 tablespoon Dijon mustard
2 dried bay leaves
2 teaspoons dried thyme
2 cups potatoes, peeled and cut in 1/2-inch pieces
2 tablespoons cornstarch, dissolved in 2 tablespoons cold water
1 1/2 cups frozen peas
1/4 cup fresh parsley, finely chopped, and divided

Pat beef pieces dry with a paper towel; sprinkle with salt and pepper. Heat oil and butter on medium high heat in a large, deep cooking pot such as a Dutch oven. Cook the beef in two batches, about 4-5 minutes, until nicely browned. Remove beef from the pot; set aside. Stir in onions, garlic and tomato paste; cook and stir 2 minutes. Add carrots and celery; cook and stir 3 minutes to brown. Add browned beef, wine, broth, vinegar, Worcestershire sauce, mustard, bay leaves, and thyme. Bring stew to a boil, reduce heat, and simmer 45 minutes. Add potatoes; simmer additional 15 minutes. Discard bay leaves. Stir in cornstarch mixture to thicken; cook 2 minutes. Stir in peas and parsley; cook 2 minutes. To serve, ladle stew into individual bowls. Making it ahead of time and warming it when ready to serve greatly enhances the flavor.

White Chicken Chili

It is guaranteed to warm your heart and soul. Fresh lime serves as an unexpected flavor brightener.

2 tablespoons butter
1 tablespoon vegetable oil
2 1/2 cups yellow or white onions, diced
2 teaspoons ground cumin
2 teaspoons dried oregano
2 large cloves garlic, minced
3 cups cooked chicken*, chopped
2 15-ounce cans cannellini beans, drained
3 cups chicken broth
1 4-ounce can diced green chiles or jalapenos
3 tablespoons fresh lime juice
1 teaspoon kosher salt
1 teaspoon coarsely ground black pepper
1/2 cup green onions, sliced thinly

Heat butter and oil in a large, deep pan. Add onions, cumin, and oregano. Cook and stir 8-10 minutes until onions are translucent and tender. Add garlic; cook 1 more minute. Stir in chicken, beans, broth, and chiles. Reduce heat; simmer 5 minutes. Add lime juice, salt, and pepper. Transfer to individual bowls and add a sprinkling of green onions for garnish. Serving suggestions: Add 1 cup frozen corn kernels at the same time you add chicken, or spoon chili over halved baked potatoes for a hearty main dish.

Cooked Chicken:

1 1/2 pounds bone-in chicken breasts and thighs
3 cups chicken broth (or enough to cover chicken pieces in the pan)
1 cup onions, chopped
2 cloves garlic, peeled and sliced
1 teaspoon kosher salt
1/2 teaspoon freshly ground black pepper

Bring broth and chicken pieces to a boil in a large saucepan. Reduce heat, and cover the pan. Simmer 10-15 minutes until chicken is opaque and internal temperature registers 165 degrees. Transfer chicken to a plate to cool. Strain broth before using it in your recipe.

Asian Pear Salad

4-6 servings

Asian pears have the taste of a pear, but the crunch of an apple. Watch for them to arrive in your grocery store mid-October and leave in late December.

Salad:
6 cups baby spinach
2 tablespoons shallots, diced
1 cup walnuts, toasted*
1 cup crumbled blue cheese
2 Asian pears, cored and thinly sliced

Balsamic Reduction Sauce:
1/2 cup balsamic vinegar
3 tablespoons honey

Apricot Dressing:
1/2 cup apricot preserves
1 teaspoon shallots, diced
1 tablespoon white wine vinegar
1/4 cup canola oil
1/4 teaspoon kosher salt
1/4 teaspoon ground black pepper

*Place walnuts in 9-inch dry skillet. Cook and stir about 3-4 minutes over medium low heat until they are fragrant and a little darker brown. Transfer to a plate; chop when cool.

Make dressing by placing all ingredients in a blender or small food processor; blend to a smooth consistency. For the reduction sauce, put the balsamic vinegar in a small saucepan. Bring to a boil; cook until it has reduced by half in volume. Add honey; bring back to a boil. Remove from heat and set aside.

Combine spinach, shallots, walnuts, and blue cheese in a bowl; lightly toss with 1/3 cup of the dressing. Set onto individual serving plates. Top with pear slices, and a drizzle of the balsamic reduction sauce. If the sauce seems a bit too thick, whisk in 1 or 2 drops of water.

Leftover dressing may be refrigerated in a glass, airtight container up to 3 days.

Cashew Chicken Salad

6-8 servings

Tired of that same old chicken salad everyone's made for years? This one has an updated twist with bright orange and apricot flavors.

Salad:
3 cups romaine lettuce, torn in small pieces
3 cups cooked chicken*, cubed in bite-sized pieces
1 1/2 cups celery, thinly sliced
3/4 cup dried apricots, diced
1 15-ounce can mandarin oranges, drained
4 green onions, thinly sliced
1 cup salted cashew halves

Orange Dressing:
1/4 cup orange (or orange pineapple) juice
1/4 cup canola oil
1/4 cup fresh parsley
1 teaspoon red wine vinegar
1 1/2 teaspoons granulated sugar
1 1/2 teaspoons Dijon mustard
1/2 teaspoon hot sauce
1/2 teaspoon kosher salt
1/4 teaspoon freshly ground black pepper

*Cooked Chicken (recipe, page 68)

Combine all salad ingredients (except cashews) in a bowl.

For the dressing, mix all ingredients in a blender or small food processor to a smooth consistency.

To finish, add dressing to the salad; stir in cashews just before serving.

COOKING with MORE CONFIDENCE

Cauliflower Almond Salad

6-8 servings

If you are looking for an out of the ordinary and unexpected salad to serve with dinner, here is one of our family favorites that will fill the bill.

1 large-sized head of cauliflower, washed thoroughly
1/2 cup dried currants
1/2 cup green onions, thinly sliced
1/2 teaspoon kosher salt
1/4 teaspoon coarsely ground black pepper
3/4 cup grated Parmesan cheese
3/4 cup slivered almonds, toasted* and chopped

Dressing:
1 tablespoon freshly grated lemon peel
1/3 cup fresh lemon juice
1/4 cup white balsamic vinegar
2 tablespoons Dijon mustard
2 tablespoons honey
1/4 cup canola oil
1 tablespoon minced shallots
1/4 teaspoon kosher salt
1/4 teaspoon coarsely ground black pepper

*Preheat oven to 350 degrees. Place almonds on a rimmed baking sheet. Bake 10-12 minutes until nuts are lightly browned and fragrant. Transfer to a cutting board to cool completely before chopping.

Cut cauliflower into small florets and place in a medium-sized bowl. Rehydrate currants in a cup of boiling water for 5 minutes; drain thoroughly, and add to the cauliflower. Add onions, salt, pepper, cheese, and chopped almonds.

Mix dressing ingredients; whisk vigorously until well blended. Add just enough dressing to the salad to coat it lightly. Serve cold or at room temperature. Because the salad doesn't have a lot of color, you may want to serve it in a bright colored bowl.

Cucumber Radish Salad

6-8 servings

Fresh and spicy radishes are showcased in this salad. Another layer of peppery flavor is added by using their green tops. You will want to use the absolutely freshest radishes you can find.

4 cups shredded romaine lettuce
3 English cucumbers, peeled and diced
1 bunch fresh radishes, thinly sliced
3 hard boiled eggs, diced
1/2 cup green onions, thinly sliced on the diagonal
1 cup feta cheese, crumbled
Green tops from the radishes - washed well, dried, and finely diced

Dressing:
1/2 cup Greek yogurt
1/2 cup sour cream
1 tablespoon fresh lemon juice
1 1/2 tablespoons fresh dill
1/2 teaspoon kosher salt
1/4 teaspoon freshly ground black pepper

Combine lettuce, cucumbers, radishes, eggs, onions, and cheese in a large bowl. Set aside the diced green radish tops for garnish.

Combine all dressing ingredients; whisk well.

Add dressing to the salad just before serving. Top with reserved radish tops.

Emma's Summer Salad

4 generous servings

When asked to make a dinner salad to accompany steaks on the grill, my granddaughter Emma came up with her own creation. Using cabbage in place of lettuce takes this salad in a new and surprising flavor direction.

3 cups shredded green cabbage
4 radishes, thinly sliced
1 large cucumber, seeded and diced
2 large carrots, shredded
2 large tomatoes, diced

Dressing:
1/2 cup mayonnaise
1/4 cup plain Greek yogurt
2 tablespoons half and half
2 tablespoons white wine vinegar
1 tablespoon whole grain mustard
1/4 teaspoon dill weed
1/4 teaspoon celery salt
1/4 teaspoon freshly ground black pepper

Combine cabbage, radishes, cucumber, carrots, and tomatoes in a large bowl.

Combine mayonnaise, yogurt, and cream; whisk well. Add vinegar, mustard, dill, celery salt, and pepper; stir to mix well. Add dressing to the salad, using just enough to coat lightly.

Cover and refrigerate until serving.

Farro Vegetable Salad

4-6 servings

My daughter-in-law Jani brought this amazing salad idea home from New York. Not familiar with farro? It is a grain with a nutty flavor similar to brown rice. Great choice for the vegetarians at your table.

1 cup farro*
1 3/4 cup apple cider
3/4 teaspoon kosher salt
2 bay leaves
1/3 cup good olive oil
2 tablespoons fresh lemon juice
1/2 cup shaved Parmesan cheese
1/2 cup pistachio nuts
1/2 cup arugula
1 cup flat leaf parsley (or fresh basil), torn in small pieces
1 cup fresh mint leaves
3/4 cup cherry tomatoes, halved
1/3 cup radishes, thinly sliced

*Look for the kind requiring a 30-minute cooking time.

Rinse farro thoroughly. Transfer to a small saucepan. Add apple cider, salt, and bay leaves. Cook, stirring occasionally, until farro is still a little firm and chewy. Remove from heat; discard bay leaves.

Mix olive oil and lemon juice; add to the cooked grain while still warm. Cool thoroughly. Stir in Parmesan cheese, pistachios, arugula, parsley, mint, tomatoes, and radishes just before serving.

COOKING WITH MORE CONFIDENCE

Fresh and Frozen Fruit Salad

8 servings

Fresh or frozen fruit may be used; however, using frozen will keep your salad refreshingly cold. The key here is the citrus dressing that pulls it all together.

Salad:
1 cup frozen cherries
1 cup frozen pineapple chunks
1 cup frozen blackberries
1 cup fresh strawberries, quartered
1 cup fresh blueberries
3 cups romaine lettuce, torn in small pieces

Dressing
1/2 cup orange juice
1/4 cup fresh lemon juice
1/4 cup canola oil
2 teaspoons granulated sugar
1 1/2 tablespoons Dijon mustard
1 tablespoon white wine vinegar
1/2 teaspoon kosher salt
1/4 teaspoon freshly ground black pepper

Combine cherries, pineapple, blackberries, strawberries, and blueberries in a large bowl. Add lettuce; stir to combine. To make dressing, whisk all ingredients together in a small, deep bowl. Because your fruit has been in a frozen state, it will give off its own juices so add the dressing sparingly.

Leftover dressing may be refrigerated in a covered glass container for up to 3 days.

Fresh Asparagus Salad

Local asparagus arrives from the field early in June. Try to find it for this recipe. Any other time of year, look for medium sized spears that are not woody in texture. Pair with Roasted Chicken and Mushrooms (recipe, page 134).

1 pound fresh asparagus (about 16-20 spears)
1 cup fresh mushrooms, thinly sliced
1/2 cup red onions, very thinly sliced
3 cups mixed salad greens of your choice
1 cup Marcona almonds, roughly chopped
1 ruby grapefruit, peeled and sectioned

Dressing:
2 tablespoons fresh shallots, minced
1 1/2 tablespoons fresh grapefruit juice
1 tablespoon champagne vinegar
1/3 cup canola oil
3/4 teaspoon Dijon mustard
1/4 teaspoon kosher salt
1/4 teaspoon freshly ground black pepper

Cut tough ends from the asparagus. Bring 2 quarts of water to a boil in a large saucepan. Add 1 1/2 teaspoons salt and 1 1/2 teaspoons of sugar to the water. Cook asparagus 2 minutes until crisp-tender; transfer immediately to a bowl of ice water to stop the cooking. Swirl asparagus around to make sure all pieces are cold.

Transfer cooked and cooled asparagus to paper towels to drain and dry. Cut in 1 1/2-inch pieces. Combine asparagus, mushrooms, onions, greens, almonds, and grapefruit in a large bowl.

Make dressing by whisking together shallots, juice, vinegar, oil, mustard, salt, and pepper. Add just enough dressing to the salad to coat lightly. Portion salad out evenly to individual plates for serving.

Italian Pasta Salad

10 servings

A colorful and tangy main dish salad, enough to feed a hungry crowd.

10 ounces mixed cheese tortellini (or substitute spinach, plain, or tomato)
4 ounces cavatappi or other firm pasta
2 cups broccoli florets
1 (14-ounce) can artichoke hearts, drained and roughly chopped
1 cup ripe olives, sliced
10-12 slices hard salami, julienned
2 cups cherry tomatoes, halved
4 green onions, sliced thinly
1/2 cup red onion, finely diced
1/2 cup Italian flat leaf parsley, finely chopped
1/2 cup fresh basil, rolled and cut in small ribbons

Dressing:
1/3 cup safflower or canola oil
1/3 cup white wine vinegar
1/4 cup fresh lemon juice
1 teaspoon kosher salt
1/2 teaspoon coarsely ground black pepper
3/4 teaspoon garlic powder

Cook tortellini and pasta according to package directions. Rinse cooked pasta with cold water. Drain well. Transfer to a large bowl, and allow to cool.

Bring 2 quarts water to a boil. Add 1 teaspoon kosher salt and 1 teaspoon granulated sugar. Add broccoli; cook 1-2 minutes until tender-crisp; drain, and cool. Combine broccoli with artichokes, olives, salami, tomatoes, and onions; mix well. Add this mixture to the drained and cooled pasta.

Combine all of the dressing ingredients; whisk well, and add to the salad. What appears to be excess dressing will absorb into the pasta. Cover, and refrigerate for at least three hours to allow flavors to blend. Add parsley and basil shortly before serving. Serve cool or at room temperature.

Lemon Drop Salad

With its lemony taste and crisp texture, this salad accompanies the Shells with Spinach and Cheese (recipe, page 89) very well.

Salad:
4 cups baby greens or romaine lettuce, torn in bite-sized pieces
1 cup pecan halves, toasted*
2 fresh pears, diced
1 sweet apple (such as Honeycrisp), diced
1/2 cup dried cranberries or dried cherries
1 cup feta cheese, crumbled

Dressing:
1/3 cup fresh lemon juice
1/2 cup granulated sugar
2 teaspoons shallots, finely chopped
2 teaspoons Dijon mustard
1/2 teaspoon kosher salt
1/4 teaspoon freshly ground black pepper
2/3 cup canola oil

*To toast pecans, place in a dry skillet over medium heat. Cook and stir pecans 2-3 minutes until they are fragrant and medium brown in color. Remove from heat; transfer to a plate to cool.

To make the dressing, place lemon juice, sugar, shallots, mustard, salt, and pepper in a blender; pulse to mix well. Slowly add oil; blend until smooth and creamy.

When ready to serve, combine all salad ingredients in a bowl; add dressing to coat lightly. The lemon juice in the dressing will keep the pears and apples from darkening.

Any leftover dressing may be refrigerated in a covered glass container up to 3 days.

Roasted Pear Salad

8 servings

Pears. Walnuts. Blue Cheese. Cranberries. What a delightful blend of flavors, all in one serving.

1/2 cup apple cider
1/3 cup brown sugar, packed
3 tablespoons ruby port wine
4 firm Bosc or Anjou pears
3 tablespoons fresh lemon juice
1/3 cup dried cranberries
1/3 cup walnuts, roasted* and chopped
1 cup crumbled blue cheese (about 4 ounces)
4 cups fresh spinach, washed and dried
2 tablespoons good olive oil
1 tablespoon balsamic vinegar
1/4 teaspoon freshly ground black pepper
1/8 teaspoon kosher salt

Preheat oven to 375 degrees.

Mix cider, sugar, and port wine until sugar has dissolved; set aside.

Peel pears; cut each in half lengthwise. Use a melon baller to remove core; cut stem out with a knife. Cut a small piece off the bottom of pear halves so they will sit flat. Gently toss pears with lemon juice; place in a glass 9 x 13-inch baking dish. Mix cranberries, walnuts, and cheese; press about 3 tablespoons into each pear cavity. Pour reserved cider mixture over the pears. Bake 30 minutes. Transfer pears to a plate from the baking dish with a slotted spoon, reserving juices. Allow pears to cool to room temperature. Mix reserved juices from the pan, olive oil, vinegar, pepper, and salt; toss lightly with spinach. To serve, divide dressed spinach between individual salad plates. Top with the filled pear halves.

*Place walnuts in 9-inch dry skillet. Cook and stir about 2-3 minutes over medium low heat until they are fragrant and a little darker brown. Transfer to a plate; chop when cool.

Scoops of Confidence

For Soups and Salads

Bring frozen soup to room temperature before reheating. Using a heavy pot on your stovetop for this task is wise. Generally speaking, microwaving soup will compromise texture and taste.

Fresh herbs bring out the best flavor and natural sweetness of vegetables. Certainly dried herbs work as well, but make sure they have not been in your pantry too long. Dried herbs lose their efficacy after about two years. Check your supply periodically. Rub dried herbs between your fingers to release natural oils and wake up their flavor. It is the best way to check for freshness.

Your salad dressing should taste good enough to drink or eat with a spoon.

Use about half the amount of dressing you think you need for a salad, and toss. Too much is too much. Sometimes, just a touch of fresh lemon juice can brighten flavors.

Use seasonal produce and/or berries whenever possible. The faster your ingredients' trip from a farm or garden to your table, the better. Buy local whenever you can. You will taste the difference.

Celery rescue: Place limp celery in ice water with 2 tablespoons of sugar for one hour. Magic.

Rehydrate dried tomatoes in boiling water for 15 minutes or cover with oil and let stand overnight before using. Tomatoes in oil are generally sweeter and more flavorful.

Go light on adding any kind of pasta or grain to your soup. They expand exponentially in liquid. This is especially important if you wish to make soup in advance and hold it in the refrigerator.

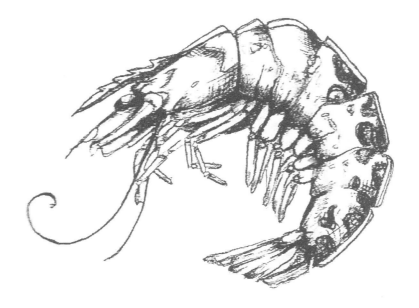

Penaeus monodon

(black tiger tail shrimp)

Pasta and Rice

Bacon Cheese Tortellini
Baked Mac 'n Cheese
Chicken Fettuccini Casserole
Creamy Rigatoni
Lemon Penne with Shrimp
Ragú Bolognese
Shells with Spinach and Cheese
Spaghetti Chicken Carbonara

Chicken Rice Bake
Creamy Ham Arancini
Plum Sauced Chicken and Rice
Rice for Supper
Wild and Brown Rice Pilaf

Scoops of Confidence

Bacon Cheese Tortellini

6-8 servings

A simple main course you will choose for those times when schedules are tight. It goes together in a manner of minutes, yet tastes like you worked all day in the kitchen.

1 20-ounce package refrigerated, mixed cheese tortellini
3 tablespoons butter
8 strips lean bacon, cut crosswise into 1/4-inch pieces
8 ounces baby bella mushrooms, sliced
1/2 cup dry sherry
1 cup half and half
1/4 teaspoon kosher salt
1/4 teaspoon freshly ground black pepper
1/4 teaspoon red pepper flakes
2 tablespoons green onions, thinly sliced
1 cup freshly grated Parmigiano Reggiano cheese*

Cook tortellini according to directions on package; drain, and keep warm.

Melt butter in a large skillet over medium heat. Add bacon; cook and stir 3 minutes until crispy. Add mushrooms; cook and stir 2 minutes. Reduce heat to low. Stir in cooked tortellini.

Add sherry, cream, salt, black pepper, and red pepper flakes; gently stir to combine. Simmer 3 minutes. Remove from the heat.

Stir in green onions and cheese; mix well. Serve immediately.

*This is not the time to use that green container of shaky cheese. The real deal makes a real difference.

Baked Mac 'n Cheese

Photograph, page 108   8 servings

Never, no never, use one of those boxed options full of preservatives and lacking in taste. This one is for real. Real ingredients, real taste. You don't even have to pre-cook the pasta.

Mac 'n Cheese:
2 cups milk
2 cups heavy cream
1 cup sour cream
2 tablespoons Dijon mustard
2 teaspoons kosher salt
1 teaspoon ground black pepper
1/4 teaspoon cayenne pepper
1/8 teaspoon nutmeg
1/4 cup butter
3 tablespoons shallots, finely diced
2 cloves garlic, minced
1/4 cup all-purpose flour
1 pound dry elbow macaroni
1 cup sharp cheddar cheese, shredded
1/2 cup fontina cheese, grated
1/2 cup Gruyère cheese, grated

Topping:
1 1/2 cups panko bread crumbs
3 tablespoons butter, melted
2 tablespoons parsley, finely chopped
1/4 cup Parmesan cheese, grated

Preheat oven to 375 degrees. Coat a 9 x 13 x 2-inch baking dish with non-stick cooking spray; set aside. Whisk milk, cream, sour cream, mustard, salt, pepper, cayenne, and nutmeg until well blended; set aside. Melt the butter in a Dutch oven over medium heat. Add shallots and garlic; cook and stir 2 minutes. Whisk in flour. Gradually add in milk mixture; whisk until smooth. Stir in dry macaroni.

Mix cheddar, fontina, and Gruyère cheeses together. Layer 1/2 of macaroni and sauce mixture in bottom of prepared dish; distribute half of the cheese mixture on top of macaroni. Repeat layers. It will look "soupy" at this point, but you will need all of this moisture to cook the macaroni. Cover the dish tightly with foil and bake 45 minutes. Remove dish from the oven. Remove foil.

Mix bread crumbs, melted butter, and parsley; distribute on top of casserole. Sprinkle with Parmesan cheese. Return dish to oven; bake (uncovered) 10 minutes. Now you have to restrain yourself - this dish needs to rest 10 minutes before serving.

Chicken Fettuccine Casserole

4 servings

When you have only a few minutes to get dinner on the table, this is a simple solution. Pretty basic ingredients, but the outcome (in less than 30 minutes) is fabulous.

8 ounces dried fettuccine pasta
1 tablespoon butter
2 tablespoons onions, diced
8 ounces button mushrooms, sliced
3 cloves garlic, minced
1 14-ounce can artichoke hearts, drained and quartered, with juice reserved
1/4 teaspoon celery salt
1/4 teaspoon freshly ground black pepper
1/4 teaspoon dried oregano
1 cup chicken broth
2 tablespoons dry white wine
1 1/2 cups cooked chicken*, cubed
3/4 cup panko bread crumbs
1/4 cup butter, melted
1/3 cup grated Parmesan cheese
1 tablespoon flat leaf parsley, minced

Preheat oven to 350 degrees.

Lightly coat a 1 1/2-quart shallow baking dish with non-stick cooking spray; set aside. Cook pasta according to directions on the package; drain and keep warm. Melt butter in a skillet over medium heat. Add onions and mushrooms; cook and stir 2 minutes. Add garlic; cook 1 minute. Add drained and quartered artichoke hearts.

Combine juice from the artichoke hearts, celery salt, pepper, oregano, broth, and wine; pour into baking dish. Spread cooked pasta over the bottom of the dish. Distribute chicken pieces on top of the pasta. Spoon mushroom mixture on top of chicken. Mix bread crumbs with butter, cheese, and parsley; sprinkle on top of the casserole. Bake 15 minutes until top has browned and dish has heated through. Serve immediately.

*Cooked Chicken (recipe, page 68)

Creamy Rigatoni

4-6 servings

While looking and tasting like gourmet fare, this wonderful pasta dish requires just a few minutes to prepare.

8 ounces dry rigatoni pasta
2 tablespoons butter
1 tablespoon canola oil
8 ounces hot Italian sausage
1/2 cup onions, diced
2/3 cup celery, diced
8 ounces fresh baby bella or button mushrooms, sliced
3 cloves garlic, minced
3 tablespoons sun-dried tomatoes in oil, finely chopped
1 cup whole milk
3 tablespoons cream cheese
1/2 teaspoon kosher salt
1/4 teaspoon dried thyme
1/4 teaspoon dried oregano
1/4 teaspoon freshly ground black pepper
1/4 teaspoon red pepper flakes
1 1/2 cups cherry tomatoes, halved
1/2 cup grated Asiago cheese
1/2 cup grated Parmesan cheese
2 tablespoons fresh parsley, finely sliced

Cook pasta according to directions on package. Drain, and keep warm.

Melt butter in a large skillet or Dutch oven over medium heat. Add sausage, using a wooden spoon to break down into crumbles. Cook and stir 3 minutes until nicely browned. Add onions and celery; cook and stir 2 minutes until crisp-tender. Add mushrooms, garlic and sun-dried tomatoes; cook and stir 2 minutes. Reduce heat to low. Mix in milk and cream cheese until sauce is thick and creamy. Add salt, thyme, oregano, black and red peppers; mix well. Add cooked pasta; simmer 3 minutes. Remove from heat. Stir in cherry tomatoes, Asiago cheese, Parmesan cheese, and 1 tablespoon parsley. Serve hot; garnish with remaining parsley.

Lemon Penne with Shrimp

Shrimp and fresh lemons are a great pair in this divine pasta dish, just right for a summertime dinner on the patio.

8 ounces dried penne pasta
2 tablespoons good olive oil
1 tablespoon butter
1/3 cup red or orange bell peppers, finely diced
4 large cloves garlic, minced
1/3 cup fresh lemon juice
1 cup chicken broth
1 pound (26-30 count) shrimp, peeled and deveined
1 1/2 teaspoons cornstarch
1 cup heavy cream
2 tablespoons freshly grated lemon peel
1/2 cup green onions, finely sliced on the diagonal
1 1/2 tablespoons fresh parsley, minced
3/4 teaspoon kosher salt
1/2 teaspoon coarsely ground black pepper
1/8 teaspoon red pepper flakes

Cook pasta according to directions on the package.

Heat oil and butter in a large skillet over medium heat. Add peppers; cook 2 minutes until tender. Add garlic; cook and stir 1 minute until fragrant. Whisk in lemon juice and broth; bring to a boil. Add shrimp; cook and stir 2 minutes until shrimp are pink and opaque. Spoon shrimp into a bowl; set aside. Whisk cornstarch and cream together; add a small amount of the warm sauce from the skillet and mix well. Pour the cream and cornstarch mixture into the skillet; whisk until thickened. Reduce heat to low. Add shrimp back to the sauce. Stir in lemon peel, green onions, parsley, salt, black and red peppers. Simmer for 3 minutes. Add cooked and warm pasta to the skillet; toss to coat with sauce. Serve immediately.

Ragú Bolognese

This sauce is very versatile, and well worth your time and effort to make from scratch. It works in a myriad of Italian based pasta dishes. Make this a day ahead because the flavors will deepen over time enriching the sauce. You will not buy the jarred stuff again.

4 slices bacon, cut in 1/4-inch pieces

3 tablespoons butter

1 1/2 cups onions, diced

3/4 cup carrots, diced

3/4 cup celery, diced

4 ounces fresh mushrooms, minced

2 cloves garlic, minced

1 pound ground beef

3/4 pound ground pork

1 3/4 teaspoons kosher salt

1/2 teaspoon black pepper

1/2 teaspoon dried thyme

1/4 teaspoon dried oregano

2 tablespoons tomato paste

1 cup dry red wine

2 (14-ounce) cans tomatoes

1 (14-ounce) can tomato sauce

1 cup beef broth

1 teaspoon granulated sugar

1/4 cup heavy cream

1/8 teaspoon crushed red pepper flakes

4 tablespoons fresh parsley, minced

Fry bacon until crispy. Add butter, onions, carrots, and celery; cook and stir about 5 minutes until vegetables are translucent. Stir in mushrooms and garlic; cook for 1 minute. Transfer vegetables to a bowl; set aside.

Return pan to the heat. Add beef and pork; use a fork or potato masher to break the meat into very small pieces. Add salt, pepper, thyme, and oregano; cook and stir until meat has browned. Add reserved vegetables back to the meat mixture, along with tomato paste, wine, tomatoes, and tomato sauce, beef broth, and sugar. Simmer 45 minutes. Stir in cream, red pepper and parsley; cook additional 10 minutes on low heat.

Shells with Spinach and Cheese

6-8 servings

Start your dish with the Lemon Drop Salad (recipe, page 78); serve these for a main dish. Wonderful.

1 16-ounce package large pasta shells
4 cups Ragú Bolognese* (recipe, page 88)
1 10-ounce package frozen spinach, thawed
2 cups ricotta cheese
2 cups shredded mozzarella cheese
1 cup grated Parmesan cheese, divided

Preheat oven to 350 degrees.

Lightly coat the inside of a 9 x 13 x 2-inch baking dish with non-stick cooking spray; set aside. Cook pasta shells according to directions on the package. Drain; keep covered to await filling. Drain thawed spinach. Using paper towels, squeeze moisture from the spinach until dry.

In a medium sized bowl, combine bolognese, spinach, ricotta cheese, mozzarella cheese, and 1/2 cup Parmesan cheese; mix thoroughly. Fill each pasta shell with 1 1/2 tablespoons of the spinach and cheese mixture. Spoon 1 cup sauce evenly into prepared baking dish. Arrange shells (stuffing side up) on the layer of sauce. Spoon remaining sauce over the shells; sprinkle with remaining Parmesan cheese.

Cover casserole with foil. Bake 30 minutes; uncover, and bake additional 10 minutes. Serve hot.

*You can also use a 32-ounce jar of quality spaghetti sauce, but you will then want to add 1/2 cup diced onions, 2 cloves minced garlic, fresh parsley, more Italian seasonings, and a little hot sauce to get it up to speed in terms of flavor.

This dish can be prepared a day ahead of time. Cool, cover, and refrigerate. Bring to room temperature before baking. This may also be frozen successfully in a glass, airtight container. Allow 1 hour and 20 minutes baking time if it's going directly from the freezer to your oven.

Spaghetti Chicken Carbonara

6 servings

It is quite likely you have everything you need on hand. Gather and go forth.

8 strips bacon, diced
3/4 pound uncooked chicken breast, cut in 1/2-inch pieces
1/3 cup dry white wine
1/2 cup chicken broth
1 1/2 tablespoons fresh lemon juice
2 eggs
1/3 cup half and half
1/2 teaspoon freshly ground black pepper
1/2 cup Parmesan cheese, grated
12 ounces dry spaghetti
1 cup frozen peas
1 tablespoon fresh parsley, minced, for garnish
1/2 teaspoon kosher salt and 1/4 teaspoon pepper

In a large, deep skillet over medium heat, cook bacon until crisp; transfer to a paper towel lined bowl to drain. Remove all but about 1 tablespoon of the bacon drippings. Add chicken; cook and stir 3-4 minutes until opaque. Transfer chicken to the bowl with reserved bacon. Add wine, broth, and lemon juice; scrape all the brown bits from the bottom of the pan. Cook and stir 3 minutes over medium heat; set aside.

In a medium bowl, whisk eggs and cream until well blended. Add pepper and cheese; stir well. Set aside. Cook spaghetti according to package directions. Just before the pasta is done, put frozen peas in a colander. Drain cooked pasta through the peas, and return pasta and peas to the warm cooking pot.

To finish, combine reserved bacon and chicken with the egg and cream mixture; stir well, and add to warm pasta. Toss well to coat evenly. Taste. Depending on how salty your bacon was, you may or may not want to add a little kosher salt at this point. Serve hot.

COOKING with MORE CONFIDENCE

Chicken Rice Bake

6-8 servings

Creamy, crunchy, comfort food that is certainly company worthy. Great served with Citrus Almond Mousse (recipe, page 176).

2 tablespoons butter
2/3 cup slivered almonds
6 strips of bacon, cut crosswise in 1/4-inch strips
3/4 cup onions, diced
3/4 cup carrots, diced
3/4 cup celery, diced
8 ounces baby bella or button mushrooms, sliced
3 cloves garlic, minced
2 teaspoons kosher salt
1 1/2 teaspoons freshly ground black pepper
4 cups cooked rice (any combination of white, brown, and/or wild)
3 cups cooked chicken*, cut in 1/2 inch pieces
2 cups sour cream
2 tablespoons fresh lemon juice
1/4 cup fresh parsley, minced
1 teaspoon dried thyme
1 cup freshly shredded Monterey Jack cheese
1/2 cup freshly grated Parmesan cheese

Preheat oven to 400 degrees. Coat a 2-quart baking dish with non-stick cooking spray; set aside. First of all, notice the recipe calls for cooked rice. You will want to do this before you start making the dish. Melt butter in a Dutch oven or a large skillet over medium heat. Add almonds; cook and stir for about a minute until they are light brown in color. Transfer almonds to a dish to cool. Add bacon pieces to the pan; cook and stir 3 minutes until crispy. Add onions, carrots, celery, and mushrooms; cook and stir 3-4 minutes until vegetables are tender-crisp. Stir in garlic, salt, and pepper; cook 1 minute. Add rice, chicken, sour cream, lemon juice, parsley, thyme, and reserved almonds; stir to mix well.

Spoon mixture into prepared baking dish. Combine Monterey Jack and Parmesan cheese; sprinkle evenly on top of rice and vegetable mixture. Bake 25 minutes. Serve hot.

*Cooked Chicken (recipe, page 68)

Creamy Ham Arancini

Photograph, page 111   *6-8 servings*

I served these arancini (Italian rice balls) at a women's luncheon with Asian Pear Salad (recipe, page 69) and Citrus Almond Mousse (recipe, page 176). Great reviews.

1 tablespoon butter
1 tablespoon vegetable oil
3/4 cup onions, finely diced
2/3 cup ham, finely diced
1 cup uncooked jasmine rice
1/2 cup dry white wine
2 1/2 cups chicken broth
1/2 teaspoon kosher salt
1/2 teaspoon ground black pepper
1/2 teaspoon dried oregano
1/4 teaspoon cayenne pepper
2/3 cup frozen green peas
3 tablespoons fresh parsley, minced

2/3 cup Parmesan cheese, grated
3 ounces mozzarella cheese
3/4 cup all-purpose flour
1/2 teaspoon kosher salt
1/2 teaspoon black pepper
2 eggs, beaten
1 1/2 cups panko bread crumbs
3 cups vegetable oil for frying

Heat butter and oil over medium heat in a 4 1/2-quart Dutch oven or heavy saucepan. Add onions; cook and stir 3 minutes. Stir in ham; cook 1 minute. Add rice; cook and stir until rice is totally coated. Add wine; stir until most of the wine has evaporated. Stir in broth, salt, pepper, oregano, and cayenne pepper; simmer, uncovered, 14 minutes. Transfer rice to a large bowl and cool for 20 minutes. Stir in peas, parsley, and Parmesan cheese.

Preheat oven to 200 degrees. Prepare 2 sheet pans, one covered with foil for the oven and one covered with layers of paper toweling to drain the rice balls once they're cooked. Set up a breading station with flour, salt, and pepper in one dish, eggs in another, and bread crumbs in another. Cut mozzarella cheese into 3/4-inch cubes. Gather 1/4 cup of the rice mixture in your hand. Place the mozzarella piece in the center, and press into a ball. Flour each, dip in egg, and cover with crumbs.

Prepare all of the balls. Heat oil in the Dutch oven to about 375 degrees. Add rice balls, a few at a time, browning on all sides. Place on towel lined pan to drain. Transfer to foil covered pan; bake 20 minutes. Serve warm.

Plum Sauced Chicken and Rice

6 servings

Rich, sweet and sour plum sauce is a key ingredient. Look for it in the Asian section of your grocery store. Paired with soy, fresh ginger and lemon, it magically transforms regular chicken and rice.

3 pounds boneless, skinless chicken breasts
4 tablespoons soy sauce, divided
3 tablespoons canola oil
1 cup onions, diced
2 cloves garlic, minced
2 teaspoons grated fresh ginger
2/3 cup plum sauce
1/2 cup frozen lemonade concentrate
1/2 cup chile sauce
3 tablespoons fresh lemon juice
2 teaspoons dry mustard
1 1/2 cup cashews
1 1/2 cups snow peas, trimmed
1 cup medium grain (such as Arborio) rice, cooked and kept hot

Preheat oven to 350 degrees. Lightly coat a 9 x 13 x 2-inch baking dish with non-stick cooking spray; set aside. Cut chicken breasts into bite size pieces; transfer to a bowl. Add 2 tablespoons soy sauce to the chicken; stir well to combine. Cover bowl with plastic wrap; refrigerate 15 minutes. Transfer chicken to a paper towel-lined plate; pat dry.

Heat oil in a skillet over medium heat. Cook and stir chicken pieces 4 minutes. Transfer chicken to prepared baking dish. Add onions to the skillet; cook and stir 1 minute. Add garlic and ginger; cook 1 more minute. Whisk in plum sauce, lemonade concentrate, chili sauce, lemon juice, mustard, and remaining soy sauce. Bring mixture to a boil. Reduce heat, cover, and simmer 3 minutes. Stir in cashews. Spoon evenly over chicken. Bake 30 minutes.

Bring 3 cups of water to a boil; add 1 teaspoon kosher salt. Cook snow peas for 2 minutes; drain, and set aside. Cook rice according to package directions. Spoon chicken over hot cooked rice. Add a few snow peas on top of each serving.

Rice for Supper

As a teenager, I made this often, except we used our own canned tomatoes from the cellar shelf and onions from the garden. We called this Spanish Rice back in the day. If you have an extra person or two at your table, simply stir in more celery, onions, and chicken broth. The dish itself is simple and very forgiving.

8 slices bacon, finely diced
1 pound ground beef
3/4 cup onions, diced
3/4 cup celery, sliced
2 cloves garlic, minced
1 1/4 cups medium grain rice
2 14-ounce cans diced tomatoes
1 cup tomato sauce
1 1/2 cups chicken broth
1 1/2 teaspoons sweet Hungarian paprika
1/2 teaspoon kosher salt
1/2 teaspoon coarsely ground black pepper

Preheat oven to 350 degrees. Butter a 2-quart baking dish; set aside.

In a large skillet over medium heat, cook and stir diced bacon and ground beef 5-7 minutes until bacon is crisp and beef has browned - use a wooden spoon to break up the beef to large crumbles. Add onions and celery; cook and stir 3 minutes. Mix in rice, tomatoes, tomato sauce, broth, salt, pepper, and paprika. Simmer 3 minutes. Transfer to prepared casserole dish. Mixture will appear to have too much liquid, but don't worry. It will be absorbed by rice in the cooking process.

Bake 25 minutes; serve while hot.

Wild and Brown Rice Pilaf

4 servings

When you need to round out your menu with a pretty looking side dish, use this one. Try it with Chicken Picatta (recipe, page 131) or Venison Swiss Steak (recipe, page 147).

3 tablespoons butter
1 cup celery, thinly sliced
1 cup onions, diced
1 cup mushrooms, sliced
1/4 cup red or orange bell peppers, finely diced
1 cup chicken broth
1/2 cup dry white wine
1 cup cooked wild rice
1 cup cooked brown rice
1/2 teaspoon kosher salt
1/2 teaspoon coarsely ground black pepper
1/8 teaspoon cayenne pepper

Melt butter in a large skillet over medium heat. Add celery and onions; cook and stir 3-4 minutes until vegetables are tender. Add mushrooms and peppers; cook and stir for 3 minutes. Reduce heat to low. Add broth and wine; simmer 5 minutes.

Stir in wild and brown rice, salt, black and cayenne peppers. Simmer 5 minutes, stirring occasionally. Serve hot.

Scoops of Confidence

For Pasta and Rice

Pasta Tips:

How much salt? Generally speaking, add 1 1/2 teaspoons kosher or sea salt per quart of cooking water. Salt is not added to pasta when it's made initially so, unless salt is added, your pasta will be flavorless.

As soon as pasta is added to the boiling, salted water, stir for a minute or so to keep the pasta from sticking together. As soon as the water comes back to a boil, the motion of the water will keep the pasta moving and keep it from sticking together - so scientifically, adding oil isn't the answer - motion is.

Reserving some of the cooking water from your pasta is a great idea. It's already seasoned, and can lighten a pasta sauce in seconds.

Rinsing cooked pasta is only necessary if you want to use it in a cold salad.

Follow cooking directions on your package of pasta; however, take a sample bite about a minute or so before it's supposed to be done. When cooked perfectly, pasta should still be a bit chewy in the center.

Rice Tips:

Type of Rice	Known As	Best Use
Short grain- length is less than two times the width	Sushi, Pearl	rice pudding, sushi, stir fry
Medium grain - length is about two times the width	Arborio	risotto, rice salads
Long grain - length is at least three times the width	Basmati, Jasmine	rice pilaf, side dishes

Check the size of your saucepan when cooking rice. When filled with uncooked rice and its cooking liquid, the saucepan should only be half full.

If you're looking for a fluffy-like rice for a side dish, remember that rinsing rice before cooking removes much of the exterior starch, preventing grains from sticking together. Place rice in a bowl, cover with cold water, and swish. Repeat until water is clear, and cook as directed.

COOKING WITH MORE CONFIDENCE

Chicken Broccoli Stir Fry

PAGE 130

Lemon Cheesecake

PAGE 171

Pork with Roasted Grapes

PAGE 138

Crunchy Granola

PAGES 41

Wildwood's Wild Rice Quiche

PAGE 49

Stuffed Mushrooms

PAGES 33

Apple Cheesecake Bars

PAGE 184

Date Night Beef Wellingtons

PAGE 142-143

Lemon Cream Double Deckers

PAGE 183

Cherry Berry Cobbler

PAGE 175

Shepherd's Pie

PAGE 144

Baked Mac 'n Cheese

PAGE 84

Horseradish Crusted Salmon

PAGE 119

Potato Bacon Chowder

PAGE 64

Creamy Ham Arancini

PAGES 92

Apricot Brandy Poundcake

PAGE 163

Salmo salar

(salmon)

Fish and Seafood

Asian Tuna Steaks
Capered Tomato Halibut
Coconut Orange Shrimp
Grouper Macadamia
Horseradish Crusted Salmon
Italian Shrimp and Pasta
Marinated Salmon Steaks
Nut Encrusted Walleye
Parmesan Lemon Walleye
Seafood Casserole
Shrimp and Corn Fritters

Scoops of Confidence

COOKING with MORE CONFIDENCE

Asian Tuna Steaks

An oh-so-simple, oh-so-good way to enjoy fresh tuna. By starting the marinade process in the afternoon, they can be finished in less than 15 minutes for your evening meal.

2 fresh tuna steaks, cut 1 to 1 1/2-inches thick

Marinade:
1/4 cup low-sodium soy sauce
1/4 cup brown sugar, packed
2 tablespoons dry sherry (not cooking sherry)
2 tablespoons rice vinegar
2 tablespoons vegetable oil
2 teaspoons toasted sesame oil
6 cloves garlic, minced
2-inch piece fresh ginger, peeled and chopped
4 green onions, finely chopped
1/8 teaspoon red pepper flakes

In a medium-sized bowl, whisk soy sauce and brown sugar together until sugar has dissolved. Add sherry, vinegar, vegetable and sesame oils; whisk well to combine. Stir in garlic, ginger, onions, and red pepper flakes. Place tuna steaks in a heavy duty zip top bag; add marinade. Refrigerate 1 1/2 hours. Turn the bag over midway through this process to make sure steaks have equal contact with the marinade.

To finish, the steaks may be broiled in your oven or grilled. In either case, remove steaks from the marinade; dry surfaces with a paper towel. Allow 2-4 minutes (depending on thickness) per side. They are meant to be served a little charred on the outside and rare on the inside. Do not overcook.

Capered Tomato Halibut

4 servings

Fish and tomatoes go hand-in-hand to make this quick and easy dinner dish. Wonderful served with Creamy Mashed Potatoes (recipe, page 157).

Tomato Sauce:
2 cups grape tomatoes, halved
2 tablespoons capers, rinsed, drained
1 1/2 teaspoons dried oregano
1/2 teaspoon kosher salt
1/4 teaspoon dried thyme
1/4 teaspoon freshly ground black pepper
Fish:
1 1/2 pounds halibut*
3/4 teaspoon kosher salt
1/4 teaspoon freshly ground black pepper
1/2 cup all-purpose flour
2 tablespoons good olive oil
2 large cloves garlic, minced

Preheat oven to 450 degrees. Yes, this is the right temperature.

In a medium bowl, mix tomatoes, capers, oregano, salt, thyme, and pepper; stir well, and set aside. Cut halibut into 4 even-sized serving pieces. Mix salt and pepper; sprinkle all sides of the fish. Dredge tops and bottoms of halibut with flour; shake off excess.

Heat oil in a large, ovenproof skillet over medium high heat until very hot (but not smoking). Add fish; cook 3 minutes on the first side. Do not move the fish until it is browned releases easily from the pan. Flip pieces over, and brown the other side. Turn heat off. Move fish to one side; stir in garlic and cook for 1 minute. Stir cooked garlic into reserved tomato mixture. Reposition fish evenly in the pan. (For even baking, make sure they do not touch each other.) Spoon tomato mixture evenly around the fish pieces. Transfer skillet to the oven; roast 4-5 minutes - time will vary depending on the thickness of the fish. Test to make sure it is firm to the touch and opaque in the center (test with a small, sharp knife). Remove skillet from the oven. Cover; let rest 2-3 minutes. To serve, spoon some of the pan juices on each plate. Place the halibut in the center; spoon tomato mixture on top and around each serving.

*This recipe will work with any mild, thick white fish (such as cod, grouper, or sea bass).

Coconut Orange Shrimp

4 servings

You will love the taste and presentation. The dipping sauce is stellar.

1 pound (16-20 count) large shrimp, peeled (leave tail intact), and deveined
1/2 cup cornstarch
1 teaspoon kosher salt
1/2 teaspoon cayenne pepper
2 egg whites, lightly beaten
2 tablespoons water
1 cup unsweetened coconut flakes
1 cup panko bread crumbs
3/4 teaspoon kosher salt
Vegetable oil for frying

Orange Dipping Sauce:
1/2 cup orange marmalade
1/4 cup butter, melted
1/4 cup Dijon mustard

3 tablespoons fresh lemon juice
2 tablespoons soy sauce
1/8 teaspoon hot sauce

Mix your Orange Dipping Sauce first: Combine all ingredients; stir well, and set aside.

It is best to prep the shrimp ingredients so you can easily follow a step by step procedure: Rinse the shrimp thoroughly under cold, running water; pat dry with a paper towel. Combine cornstarch, salt, and cayenne in zip top bag. In a small bowl, whisk egg whites and water until frothy. In another zip top bag, combine coconut, bread crumbs, and salt. Set a wire rack inside a large rimmed baking sheet to accept the shrimp once it's coated.

Heat 1/2-inch oil to 365 degrees (very hot, but not smoking) in a large Dutch oven or heavy, large skillet. Put shrimp, a few at a time, in the bag with cornstarch mixture. Shake to coat; shake off excess. Dip shrimp in egg white mixture, then into the bag with the coconut. Fry in batches - 1 to 2 minutes per side. Transfer to prepared rack. Serve hot, with Orange Dipping Sauce.

Grouper Macadamia

After a delightful morning on the water, dear Florida friends, here's dinner with your catch of the day.

4 grouper fillets
1 cup macadamia nuts
2 slices day-old French or country bread
2 tablespoons shallots, minced
2 tablespoons flat leaf parsley, minced
1/4 cup coarse grain mustard
2 tablespoons fresh lime juice
1/4 teaspoon hot sauce

Preheat oven to 350 degrees. Place a wire rack inside a rimmed baking pan; set aside.

Toast macadamia nuts by placing them on a small, rimmed baking sheet. Bake 8-10 minutes until light brown and fragrant; set aside to cool.

Increase oven temperature to 425 degrees.

Rinse fish under cold, running water; pat dry with a paper towel.

Using a food processor, pulse bread to measure 1 cup soft crumbs. Finely chop reserved macadamia nuts. Combine crumbs, nuts, shallots, and parsley. Combine mustard, lime juice, and hot sauce. Using a pastry brush, coat each fish fillet with mustard mixture. Dredge each fillet in crumb/nut mixture. Place fish on prepared baking pan.

Bake 10 minutes per 1-inch thickness of your fillets.

Horseradish Crusted Salmon

Photograph, page 109   *6-8 servings*

A memorable main dish that your guests will keep talking about weeks later.

2 1/2 pound salmon fillet
2 medium onions, thinly sliced
2 lemons, thinly sliced
1 1/2 teaspoons kosher salt
1 teaspoon freshly ground black pepper
Topping:
1 1/2 cups mayonnaise
3 tablespoons horseradish (regular or hot)
1/4 cup green onions, sliced
1 teaspoon freshly grated lemon peel
1/2 teaspoon dill weed
1/2 teaspoon freshly ground black pepper
2 tablespoons fresh parsley, minced
3/4 cup panko breadcrumbs

Preheat oven to 350 degrees.

Use a 2-piece broiler pan. Pour 1 cup water in the bottom. Coat top rack with non-stick cooking spray. Arrange sliced onions on rack to run the width and length of the salmon fillet. Season both sides of salmon with salt and pepper. Place fillet on top of the onions, folding under the tail end to make an even thickness. Cover the salmon with lemon slices. Bake 30-35 minutes (time will vary depending on the thickness of the fish). Test doneness by poking the tip of a sharp knife in the thickest part of the fillet. It should be opaque and easily flake when separated. Remove from the oven. Change oven setting from Bake to Broil. Move oven rack to within 6 inches of the broiler. Mix mayonnaise and horseradish in a medium bowl. Stir in onions, lemon peel, dill, and pepper; mix well. Stir in bread crumbs and 1 tablespoon parsley. Spread horseradish mixture evenly on top of salmon. Sprinkle with remaining parsley.

Place under the broiler. Watch carefully. Each broiler seems to work a little differently, so a constant eye on this process is very important. Broil 2-3 minutes until top is bubbly and light brown in color. Remove from the oven; let rest 5 minutes before slicing and serving.

Italian Shrimp and Pasta

4 generous servings

If you make this wonderful tasting sauce ahead of time, all you need to do before dinner is cook the pasta.

8 ounces dry pasta (such as fettucini or linguine)
1 pound raw shrimp (26-30 count), peeled and deveined (leave tails on 4)
Sauce:
1 tablespoon butter
1 tablespoon canola oil
1/4 cup grated onion
1/4 cup grated carrots
1/4 cup celery, finely diced
1 clove garlic, minced
2 tablespoons tomato paste
1 1/2 teaspoons dried Italian seasoning
1/2 teaspoon red pepper flakes
1 14-ounce can diced tomatoes, undrained
3/4 cup canned vegetable juice
1/2 cup dry red wine
1/2 cup heavy cream
3/4 teaspoon kosher salt
1/2 teaspoon freshly ground black pepper
2 tablespoons fresh parsley, minced

Put water on medium high heat for cooking pasta. When water comes to a boil, add salt and pasta. Cook according to package directions.

For the sauce, combine butter and oil in a 10-inch skillet over medium high heat. Add onions, carrots, and celery; cook and stir for 4-5 minutes until vegetables are tender and the pan is almost dry. Add garlic, tomato paste, Italian seasoning, and red pepper; cook and stir 1 minute. Stir in tomatoes, juice, and wine. Bring to a boil; reduce heat and simmer 5 minutes. Add shrimp, cover the skillet, and cook 3-4 minutes or until shrimp is opaque and pink in color. Remove from heat; stir in cream, salt, and pepper. Remove the 4 shrimp with tails. Transfer hot pasta to individual serving dishes; spoon shrimp and sauce on top. Garnish with whole shrimp and parsley. Gently rewarm the sauce over very low heat, if made ahead of time.

COOKING WITH MORE CONFIDENCE

Marinated Salmon Steaks

4 servings

The idea for this marinade comes from my friend John and his salmon-fishing brother in Alaska. Unbelieveable flavor.

4 fresh salmon steaks

Marinade:
2/3 cup low-sodium soy sauce
2/3 cup frozen limeade concentrate, thawed
2/3 cup good olive oil
2 large cloves fresh garlic, minced
2 teaspoons fresh rosemary, minced
2 teaspoons fresh ginger, grated

Whisk together the soy sauce, limeade concentrate, oil, garlic, rosemary, and ginger. Pour this mixture into a large, heavy, resealable bag. Add steaks; remove extra air from the bag. Refrigerate 1 hour.

Bring steaks to room temperature. Pat dry with a paper towel.

At this point, you may choose one of three ways to finish:

    (A) Using a buttered, ovenproof baking dish, bake in a 425 degree preheated oven for 10-12 minutes
    (B) Preheat broiler; cook 5 minutes, turn the steaks over, and cook additional 3-4 minutes
    (C) Grill on medium high heat for 5 minutes, turn the steaks over, and cook additional 3-4 minutes

Cooking time will vary depending on thickness of the steaks. Consideration must be given to the fact that fish continue to cook a little after being removed from the heat source, so watch carefully. When steaks are done, they should flake easily with a fork.

Nut Encrusted Walleye

Simply said, delicious either way.

Almond Crusted Walleye:

4 6-ounce walleye fillets
1/4 teaspoon kosher salt and 1/8 teaspoon freshly ground black pepper
3/4 cup all-purpose flour
2 eggs - lightly beaten, and mixed with 2 tablespoons milk
1 cup almonds, very finely chopped, mixed with 1 cup panko bread crumbs
2 ounces Amaretto liqueur, mixed with 1/4 cup melted butter
1/2 cup vegetable oil - mixed with 1/4 cup butter, for frying

Preheat oven to 400 degrees. Lightly coat a shallow baking dish with non-stick cooking spray. Sprinkle fillets with salt and pepper. Dust lightly with flour; shake off excess. Dip in egg mixture. Press fillets into almond mixture. Heat oil in large skillet over medium heat until very hot (but not smoking). Quickly brown fillets on both sides; transfer to prepared dish. Drizzle fillets with Amaretto and butter mixture. Bake 7-10 minutes - time will depend on thickness of fish. It should easily flake with a fork when done.

Charlie's Pecan Crusted Walleye:

4 6-ounce walleye fillets
1/4 teaspoon kosher salt
1/8 teaspoon freshly ground black pepper
3/4 cup all-purpose flour
2 eggs - lightly beaten, and mixed with 2 tablespoons milk
1/2 cup pecans, very finely chopped, mixed with:
    1/2 cup instant potato buds and 1/2 cup panko bread crumbs
1/2 cup vegetable oil - mixed with 1/4 cup butter, for frying

Sprinkle fillets with salt and pepper. Dust lightly with flour; shake off excess. Dip in egg mixture. Press fillets into pecan mixture. Heat oil in large skillet over medium heat until hot (but not smoking). Cook fillets for 2-3 minutes or until browned on bottom side; flip, and cook the other side until fish flakes easily with a fork.

Parmesan Lemon Walleye

4 servings

With help from your oven, this is a quick and delicious recipe to showcase our favorite Minnesota fish.

4 large walleye fillets
2 tablespoons fresh lemon juice
1/2 teaspoon kosher salt mixed with 1/2 teaspoon freshly ground black pepper
1/2 cup dry white wine
3 tablespoons mayonnaise
4 tablespoons butter, softened
1 cup freshly grated Parmesan cheese
Sauce:
1/2 cup heavy cream
1 tablespoon fresh lemon juice
1/2 cup butter, chilled and cut in pieces
1/8 teaspoon kosher salt
1 1/2 tablespoons fresh parsley, minced (for garnish)

Preheat oven to 400 degrees. Butter a shallow baking dish large enough to lay all fillets flat.

Brush each walleye piece with lemon juice. Sprinkle with salt and pepper. Transfer to baking dish. Add wine; set aside. Combine mayonnaise, butter, and cheese in a small bowl. Mix well; set aside.

Bake walleye and wine 10 minutes.

Remove from the oven; spread mayonnaise mixture evenly over fillets. Return dish to oven; bake 2 minutes. Remove from the oven; cover loosely with foil.

In a small skillet, bring cream and lemon juice to a boil over medium heat. Reduce heat; simmer until it has reduced by half in volume. Whisk in butter pieces, allowing each piece to melt before adding another. To serve, spoon some of the sauce on individual plates. Place walleye fillet on top of the sauce. Spoon remaining sauce over the fish and garnish with parsley.

Seafood Casserole

A lovely way to celebrate the tastes and textures of scallops and shrimp. Company worthy.

Topping:
3/4 cup panko bread crumbs
3/4 cup Gruyère cheese, grated
2 tablespoons butter

Seafood Mixture:
4 tablespoons butter
12 shrimp (26-30 count),
    peeled and deveined
12 dry pack sea scallops, halved
3/4 cup onions, diced
3/4 cup celery, diced
1 1/2 cups mushrooms, sliced
1/2 cup red bell pepper, diced
2 cloves garlic, minced

3/4 teaspoon kosher salt
1/2 teaspoon black pepper
1/4 teaspoon cayenne pepper
2/3 cup dry sherry
1/4 cup all-purpose flour
1 1/2 cup whole milk or half and half
1 tablespoon Worcestershire sauce
2 teaspoons fresh lemon juice

Preheat oven to 350 degrees.

Heat a skillet over medium low heat. Add bread crumbs. Cook and stir 1-2 minutes until crumbs turn light brown in color. Stir in butter and cheese; transfer to a dish and reserve.

Melt butter in the skillet over medium heat. Add shrimp and scallops; cook and stir 2 minutes. With a slotted spoon, remove seafood to a plate. Add onions and celery to the skillet; cook and stir 2 minutes. Add mushrooms, bell pepper, garlic, salt, pepper, and cayenne; cook and stir 2 minutes. Stir in sherry. Mix in flour; cook 1 minute. Gradually add milk; cook 2 minutes. Stir in Worcestershire, lemon juice, scallops and shrimp.

Spoon into a 1 1/2-quart baking dish. Distribute reserved topping evenly over the casserole. Bake 20 minutes until bubbly. Serve hot.

Shrimp and Corn Fritters

The combination of a warm fritter with fresh avocado cream sauce is superb.

1 pound raw shrimp - shelled, deveined, diced, and patted dry
1 tablespoon soy sauce
2 eggs
1/3 cup whole milk
1 1/4 cups flour
1/2 teaspoon kosher salt
1 cup corn kernels
1/2 cup green onions, thinly sliced
1 tablespoon sesame oil
1/2 cup vegetable oil for frying

Avocado Cream:
1 ripe avocado, peeled and pitted
1/4 cup sour cream
1/2 cup cilantro leaves and stems
1 tablespoon fresh lime juice
1/4 teaspoon kosher salt
1/4 teaspoon freshly ground black pepper

Make Avocado Cream first: Put avocado, sour cream, cilantro, lime juice, salt, and pepper in a food processor or blender; process until smooth. Reserve for serving with the fritters.

Cover a rimmed baking pan with 3 layers of paper toweling; set aside. Combine diced shrimp with soy sauce; set aside. In a medium bowl, whisk eggs, milk, flour, and salt until smooth. Add corn, onions, and sesame oil; mix well. Stir in reserved shrimp and soy sauce mixture.

Heat oil in a small, deep skillet until it is very hot but not smoking. Drop shrimp mixture by the tablespoon into the oil. Cook 3-4 minutes per side, turning with tongs or a wooden spoon to make sure all sides have evenly browned. Cook in batches - do not crowd the skillet.

Transfer cooked fritters to prepared pan to drain excess oil. Serve warm with a spoonful of Avocado Cream.

Scoops of Confidence

For Fish and Seafood

Fish Tips:

Pat fish dry with paper towels before preparing to cook.

If you need to keep fish warm before serving, preheat your oven to 275 degrees. Place fillets in a single layer on a paper towel-lined, rimmed baking sheet for up to 15 minutes. Do not cover the fish, as any coating will become soggy.

Do NOT re-freeze fish. It will lose its flavor and texture.

Seafood Tips:

Shrimp are sold according to the number of pieces per pound. The lower the number, the larger the shrimp.

Unshelled shrimp should be shiny, firm, and translucent. They should smell like the sea, and have no odor of ammonia. You will need about 1/2 pound raw, shelled shrimp per serving - or 3/4 pound unshelled. After cooking, you will end up with about 1/4 pound per serving.

Rinse with cold water, dry, cover tightly, and refrigerate fresh, uncooked shrimp up to 3 days. Cooked shrimp can be covered tightly and refrigerated up to 3 days.

For optimum flavor, cook unshelled shrimp only until they turn pink. Peeled shrimp will look opaque and will have curled slightly when done. Whatever preparation method you use, be careful not to overcook shrimp, as they will quickly become tough and rubbery.

Sea scallops are about 3 times larger than bay scallops. When you get to the fish market, I would suggest purchasing DRY scallops. They should be light beige to pinkish-orange in color. Avoid those totally white, more than likely these have been soaked in water. Refrigerate immediately after purchase, and use within 1 or 2 days. As with shrimp, take care not to overcook scallops. They cook quickly - 1 to 3 minutes total searing time.

Phasianus colchicus

(ring-necked pheasant)

Poultry, Meat, and Game

Baked Honey Mustard Chicken
Chicken Broccoli Stir Fry
Chicken Picatta
Chicken Pot Pies
Quick Chicken Cutlets
Roasted Chicken and Mushrooms
Sesame Chicken Drummies

Beer Brats, Sauerkraut Salad
Pork Loin Pockets
Pork with Roasted Grapes
Roasted Apple Pork Chops
Rosemary Port Pork Roast

All American Meatloaf
Date Night Beef Wellingtons
Shepherd's Pie

Pheasant and Wild Rice
Sauced Peppercorn Venison
Venison Swiss Steak

Scoops of Confidence

COOKING with MORE CONFIDENCE

Baked Honey Mustard Chicken

4 servings

Thighs are the most flavorful part of the chicken. Here is a simple and incredible way to prepare them.

4 bone-in chicken thighs
1 1/2 cups sour cream
1/4 cup whole-grain mustard
1 tablespoon honey
2 teaspoons lemon pepper seasoning
1/2 teaspoon paprika
1 tablespoon butter
1/2 cup panko bread crumbs
1/8 teaspoon freshly ground black pepper
1 pound wide egg noodles, cooked according to directions on the package

Preheat oven to 400 degrees. Coat a ovenproof baking dish with non-stick cooking spray; set aside.

Should the chicken thighs have skin, remove it at this time and discard. In a medium bowl, whisk together sour cream, mustard, honey, lemon pepper, and paprika until smooth. Pour into prepared baking dish. Add chicken pieces; turn to coat evenly. Bake, uncovered, 45 minutes.

Remove chicken from the baking dish and place in a shallow bowl; cover with foil. Transfer the pan juices from the baking dish to a blender; mix until smooth, and set aside.

In a small skillet over medium low heat, melt butter. Add bread crumbs and pepper. Cook and stir 1-2 minutes until crumbs are toasted.

Place hot, cooked noodles on a large serving plate. Top with chicken pieces. Spoon reserved sauce on top, and garnish with toasted bread crumbs.

Chicken Broccoli Stir Fry

Photograph, page 97   *6 servings*

My granddaughter Emma makes this dish so often she can make it with her eyes closed. Well, almost...

2 pounds boneless, chicken breasts
3 tablespoons low-sodium soy sauce
1 1/4 pounds fresh broccoli
8 ounces fresh mushrooms
1 red or orange bell pepper
1 tablespoon freshly grated ginger

5 cloves fresh garlic, minced
3 tablespoons vegetable oil, divided
1 cup roasted cashew halves
3 green onions, sliced on the diagonal
6 cups cooked rice

<u>*Sauce:*</u>

5 tablespoons oyster sauce
2 tablespoons chicken broth
1 tablespoon dry sherry

1 tablespoon dark brown sugar
1 teaspoon toasted sesame oil
1 teaspoon cornstarch

Cut chicken breasts in half lengthwise; slice into thin 1/4-inch slices and then into bite-sized pieces. Combine chicken with soy sauce in a bowl; cover bowl with plastic wrap and refrigerate for 20 minutes. Cut florets from broccoli into 3/4-inch pieces. Trim broccoli stems, peel, and cut stalks thinly on the diagonal; set aside. Cut mushrooms and peppers into 1/4-inch slices; set aside. Mix ginger, garlic, and 1 1/2 teaspoons oil in a small bowl; set aside.

For sauce, combine oyster sauce, broth, sherry, sugar, and sesame oil in a small bowl. Whisk in cornstarch until smooth; set aside.

Drain chicken pieces; blot dry with a paper towel. Heat 1 1/2 teaspoons oil in a large 12-inch non-stick skillet over high heat. Add half the chicken pieces, making one layer. Cook for 1 minute. Turn the pieces over; cook about 30 seconds until both sides are brown. Transfer chicken to a bowl. Add 1 1/2 teaspoons oil to the skillet along with remaining chicken pieces; cook as before, and transfer to the bowl. Add 1 tablespoon oil to the skillet. Add broccoli pieces; cook 30 seconds. Add 1/3 cup water; cover, and steam for 2 minutes until tender-crisp. Transfer to a paper towel-lined plate.

Add 1 1/2 teaspoons oil to the skillet. Cook and stir mushrooms over medium heat. Cook and stir mushrooms 2 minutes. Add pepper pieces; cook and stir 1 1/2 minutes. Push mushrooms and peppers off to the sides. Add garlic mixture to the center of the skillet; cook and stir 30 seconds, then combine with mushrooms and peppers. Stir in sauce, cashews, and scallions; toss and cook until sauce has thickened. Serve with hot, cooked rice.

Chicken Picatta

If you have all your ingredients prepped and ready, this economical dish can be on your dinner table in less than 10 minutes. Consider substituting pork for equally amazing results.

1 1/2 pounds boneless, skinless chicken breast
1/2 teaspoon kosher salt, mixed with 1/4 teaspoon ground black pepper
1/2 cup instant flour (such as Wondra)*
4 tablespoons good olive oil, divided
1 cup low-sodium chicken broth
2 tablespoons freshly grated lemon peel (reserve for garnish)
3 tablespoons + 2 teaspoons fresh lemon juice
2 tablespoons capers, drained
4 tablespoons flat leaf parsley, minced and divided
3 tablespoons butter, room temperature

Cut each breast in half horizontally - each half should be about 1/2-inch thick. Cut the pieces again, this time in half for even serving sizes. Place each piece between sheets of plastic wrap; pound the chicken to about a 3/8-inch thickness. Season each side with the salt and pepper mixture. Dredge chicken pieces in flour and shake off excess; set aside.

Heat a large, heavy skillet** over medium heat for about 2 minutes until very hot. Add 2 tablespoons oil; heat until very hot and shimmering. Add half of the chicken pieces; cook (without moving) 2 minutes until the undersides are nicely browned. Turn chicken over; cook additional 2 minutes. Transfer pieces to a paper towel-lined plate to drain. Add remaining oil, heat 1 minute until very hot. Add remaining chicken pieces; cook 2 minutes per side; transfer to paper towel-lined plate to drain.

Add broth and lemon juice to the skillet, scraping up any brown bits from the bottom of the pan. Cook 4-5 minutes over medium heat until liquid has reduced by about half. Turn heat off. Stir in capers and parsley. Swirl in butter; stir until melted. Transfer chicken to individual serving plates. Spoon sauce over the top; garnish with remaining parsley and reserved lemon peel.

*Using instant flour will ensure even coating of the chicken and a smooth sauce with no lumps.
**You will get optimum browning results by using a regular skillet instead of a non-stick.

Chicken Pot Pies

To impart the best homemade taste, cook your own chicken. What a difference it makes.

1/2 package frozen puff pastry sheets, thawed
1 egg, beaten, mixed with 1 tablespoon cold water
6 tablespoons butter
3/4 cup onions, finely diced
1 1/2 cups celery, finely diced
1 1/2 cups carrots, thinly sliced
1 clove garlic, minced
1 tablespoon red bell pepper, finely diced
1/2 cup all purpose flour
2 1/2 cups low-sodium chicken broth
1 1/2 teaspoons instant chicken flavored granules
1/2 teaspoon dried thyme
3/4 teaspoon kosher salt
1/2 teaspoon coarsely ground black pepper
1 1/2 teaspoons Dijon mustard
1/3 cup heavy cream
2 1/2 cups cooked chicken*, cubed
3/4 cup green peas
2 tablespoons fresh parsley, finely chopped

Preheat oven to 395 degrees. Select 6 individual ovenproof ramekins that will hold at least 1 cup; set aside. Cut out puff pastry rounds just a bit smaller than ramekins; brush with egg mixture. Transfer to a baking sheet. Bake 20-25 minutes until pastry is puffed and golden; set aside. Reduce oven temperature to 375 degrees.

Melt butter in a large, heavy pot or skillet over medium heat. Add onions, celery, and carrots; cook and stir for about 5 minutes, or until tender. Add garlic and red pepper; cook additional minute. Add flour; cook and stir for 2 minutes until mixture is golden brown. Add broth and chicken flavored granules, thyme, salt, pepper, and mustard. Bring to a boil. Stir in cream, chicken, peas, and parsley. Spoon into individual ramekins, filling each to within 1/2-inch of the top. Place baked pastry rounds on top of each pot pie. Transfer prepared pies to a rimmed baking sheet. Bake 35 minutes. Remove from the oven; let rest for 15 minutes before serving.

* Cooked Chicken (recipe, page 68)

Quick Chicken Cutlets

4 servings

Gather your ingredients and go for it. This main dish can be on your dinner table in 30 minutes. Serve with noodles, rice, or mashed potatoes.

3/4 cup slivered almonds
4 boneless, skinless chicken breast halves
1/2 teaspoon kosher salt
1/4 teaspoon freshly ground black pepper
1 egg and 2 tablespoons water
1/4 teaspoon each: dried thyme, dried rosemary, and dried oregano
1 cup panko bread crumbs
1 tablespoon canola oil
1/2 cup dry white wine
1/2 cup chicken broth
2 cloves fresh garlic, minced
2 tablespoons freshly grated lemon peel
1/2 cup fresh lemon juice
2 teaspoons cornstarch mixed with 2 teaspoons water
2 tablespoons butter
2 tablespoons fresh parsley, minced

Preheat oven to 350 degrees.

Put almonds on a rimmed baking sheet. Bake 8-10 minutes until brown on the edges and fragrant; set aside. Sandwich chicken breasts between two pieces of plastic wrap; flatten to an even thickness. Mix salt and pepper; season both sides. Whisk egg and water together; transfer to a shallow bowl. Mix thyme, rosemary, and oregano with bread crumbs; transfer mixture to another shallow bowl. Dip each seasoned chicken piece in egg mixture, shaking off excess. Dredge in seasoned bread crumbs. Heat oil in a large, ovenproof skillet over medium heat. Add chicken breasts; cook 2 minutes on each side to brown well. Transfer chicken to a plate. Deglaze the skillet with wine, scraping up all the brown bits from the bottom of the pan. Add broth, garlic, lemon peel, and juice; cook and stir 2 minutes. Whisk in cornstarch mixture; cook 2 minutes to thicken. Whisk in butter and toasted almonds.

Transfer chicken back to the pan, turning each piece to coat with sauce. Bake 10 minutes. Remove from the oven, cover; let rest 10 minutes. Garnish with parsley.

Roasted Chicken and Mushrooms

Time tested and true, here is one of those basic recipes we all need.

Oven Roasted Chicken:
One 3 1/2 to 4 pound chicken
1 1/4 teaspoons kosher salt, divided
3/4 teaspoon black pepper, divided
1/4 teaspoon dried thyme
1/4 teaspoon dried rosemary
1 tablespoon butter

Mushroom Sauce:
1 tablespoon butter
2 tablespoons shallots, diced
8 ounces fresh mushrooms, sliced
1 1/2 tablespoons all-purpose flour
pan juices from the chicken you have roasted to equal 1 cup
1/2 cup dry Marsala wine
1/4 cup heavy cream
1 teaspoon fresh parsley, minced

Preheat oven to 425 degrees. Butter the bottom of a baking dish just large enough to hold your whole chicken; set aside.

Remove the backbone and tail* from the chicken with poultry shears or a sharp knife. Turn chicken, breast side up. Using your hands, flatten the chicken slightly to an even thickness. Dry the chicken (inside and outside) with a paper towel. Mix 3/4 teaspoon salt, 1/2 teaspoon pepper, thyme, and rosemary in a small dish. Using your fingers, make small pockets under the skin. Distribute seasonings evenly under the skin. Rub the entire surface of the chicken with butter; sprinkle with remaining salt and pepper. Transfer chicken to prepared baking dish, breast side up. Add 1/3 cup water to the dish. Roast, uncovered, 15 minutes. Reduce oven temperature to 375 degrees; flip the chicken (breast side down); roast additional 25-30 minutes until internal temperature is 180 degrees and juices run clear. Remove from oven; transfer to a plate, and cover with foil to allow redistribution of juices. Let it rest while you make the mushroom sauce.

Melt butter in a skillet over medium heat. Add shallots; cook and stir 1 minute. Add mushrooms; cook and stir 4 minutes. Add flour; cook and stir 2 minutes. Whisk in pan juices (from chicken baking dish) and wine; cook 5-6 minutes to reduce by half. Stir in cream and parsley. To serve, cut chicken as desired. The mushroom sauce can either be passed separately at the table, or spooned over the chicken.

*These pieces, along with any giblets you may have gotten with your chicken, may be bagged and frozen - they come in handy if you wish to make your own chicken broth at a later date.

Sesame Chicken Drummies

6 servings

A flavorful dish you can do ahead of time. It freezes and reheats beautifully.

12 large chicken drummies (about 4 pounds)
1 teaspoon kosher salt
3/4 teaspoon freshly ground black pepper
1/2 cup all purpose flour
non-stick cooking spray
Sauce:
1 cup chicken broth
1/4 cup soy sauce
1/3 cup + 1 tablespoon honey
2 tablespoons sesame oil
2 tablespoons sherry vinegar
1 1/2 tablespoons Thai style chili sauce OR ground fresh chili paste
3 large cloves garlic, minced
2 tablespoons cornstarch mixed with 2 tablespoons cold water
Garnish:
1/2 cup sesame seeds
4 green onions, thinly sliced

Preheat oven to 400 degrees. Line a large, rimmed baking sheet with foil. Place a wire rack on the pan. Mix salt and pepper together; liberally season all sides of the drummies. Pour the flour into a large zip top bag. Add the drummies, two at a time, to the flour and shake off excess. Coat the chicken pieces lightly with non-stick cooking spray. Place on the prepared pan. Roast 30 minutes; turn drummies over, and roast additional 30 minutes.

Combine broth, soy sauce, honey, oil, vinegar, chili sauce, and garlic in a small saucepan. Bring mixture to a boil; reduce heat, and simmer 15 minutes. Combine cornstarch and water in a small bowl. Add 1/4 cup of the hot mixture; stir mixture back into the saucepan. Simmer 3 minutes.

In a small, dry non-stick skillet, cook and stir sesame seeds for about 1 minute until golden brown. Transfer roasted chicken to a serving platter. Pour sauce over the top; sprinkle with seeds and onions.

Beer Brats

Get these ready for the grill with marinade to add flavor. With a side of special Sauerkraut Salad suggested by my friend Rae, it will be a home run favorite.

12 natural casing, unseasoned bratwurst
1/4 cup Dijon mustard
1/4 cup Worcestershire sauce
2 tablespoons molasses
2 cups pale ale (2 beers, with some left for the cook)
12 large hot dog buns

Combine mustard, Worcestershire, and molasses in a medium bowl; stir well. Whisk in ale. Using a fork or the tip of a knife, poke holes in the surface of the brats. (This step will make sure some of the fat is released and marinade is absorbed.) Place the brats in a large resealable zip top bag. Add marinade; refrigerate several hours or overnight. Preheat your grill to medium. Remove brats from the marinade; dry with a paper towel. Grill brats about 8-10 minutes until cooked through. Serve on buns with Sauerkraut Salad and other condiments of your choice.

Sauerkraut Salad

Sauerkraut Salad:
2 1/2 cups refrigerated sauerkraut, rinsed in cold water and patted dry
1 cup celery, diced
1/2 cup onion, diced
1/4 cup red or orange bell pepper, diced
1/4 cup green pepper, diced

Dressing:
1/2 cup apple cider vinegar
1/2 cup vegetable oil
3/4 cup granulated sugar
1/2 teaspoon celery seed
1/4 teaspoon coarsely ground black pepper

Combine sauerkraut, celery, onions, and peppers in a medium bowl.

For the dressing, whisk vinegar, oil, sugar, celery seed, and pepper together in a small saucepan. Bring to a boil over medium low heat; cook two minutes. Remove from heat; cool to room temperature. To finish, add cooled dressing to sauerkraut mixture; mix well. Serve with marinated, cooked brats.

Pork Loin Pockets

4 generous servings

A combination of fresh vegetables, fruit, and pork that is delicious and very pretty on your plate.

4 pork loin slices, each cut 1-inch thick
1/4 cup butter, divided
3/4 teaspoon kosher salt and 1/2 teaspoon freshly ground black pepper, mixed

Stuffing:

1 cup carrots, diced	**2 cups soft bread crumbs**
1 cup celery, diced	**3/4 cup chicken broth**
1/3 cup onions, diced	**1/2 teaspoon kosher salt**
3/4 cup dried apricots, diced	**1/2 teaspoon ground black pepper**
3/4 cup unpeeled apples, diced	**1/2 teaspoon celery salt**
	1/2 teaspoon dried poultry seasoning

Preheat oven to 350 degrees. Lightly coat a 2 1/2-quart baking dish with non-stick cooking spray; set aside.

Cut a pocket in each pork slice by inserting a small, sharp knife in one side. Cut to within an inch of each side and an inch of the bottom, creating a pocket. In a skillet over medium heat, melt 2 tablespoons butter. Cook the pork slices 2 minutes on each side to brown; transfer to a plate. Sprinkle with salt and pepper mixture on all sides; transfer to a plate to cool.

Melt remaining butter in skillet. Add carrots, celery, and onions; cook and stir 3 minutes until vegetables are tender-crisp. Transfer mixture to a bowl; stir in apricots, apples, bread crumbs, broth, salt, pepper, celery salt, and poultry seasoning. Mix well.

Stuff pockets of the cooled pork slices firmly with stuffing mixture, using about 1/3 cup in each. Place pork, stuffing side up, in prepared baking dish. Spoon remaining stuffing around the edges. Cover the dish; bake 30 minutes. Adjust oven temperature to 375 degrees. Uncover dish; bake additional 15 minutes.

Allow pork pockets to rest 10 minutes. Transfer to serving plates; spoon extra stuffing on the side.

Pork with Roasted Grapes

Photograph, back cover and page 99   *6 servings*

Roasted grapes lend a note of amazing interest to this main dish. It's one of my all time favorites.

1 pound unflavored pork tenderloin
1/4 cup balsamic vinegar
1 tablespoon canola oil
2 tablespoons whole grain mustard
2 teaspoons fresh rosemary, finely chopped
2 teaspoons green onions, sliced
1/2 teaspoon kosher salt
1/2 teaspoon freshly ground black pepper
1 pound red seedless grapes
2 teaspoons good olive oil
3/4 teaspoon freshly ground black pepper
1 teaspoon fresh rosemary, finely chopped
A few sprigs of fresh rosemary for garnish

In a small bowl, whisk vinegar, oil, mustard, rosemary, and onions together for a marinade. Place marinade in a large resealable bag; add tenderloin, and refrigerate 2 hours. Remove from refrigerator; allow to stand at room temperature for 15 minutes while you preheat oven to 425 degrees.

Lightly coat a shallow, oblong baking dish with non-stick cooking spray. Remove tenderloin from marinade; season with salt and pepper, and place in prepared dish. Roast 15 minutes.

While still on the vine, cut the grapes into small clusters. Toss lightly with oil, pepper, and rosemary.

Remove tenderloin from the oven. Nestle grape clusters next to the pork. Return dish to the oven, and roast additional 10 minutes until meat registers 145 degrees. (Grapes will be light colored and plump.) Cover with foil; allow 10 minutes resting time to redistribute juices. Slice; serve with pan juices and grapes. Garnish with sprigs of rosemary.

Roasted Apple Pork Chops

4 servings

Apples, onions, cider and cream turn an ordinary dish into a sensational entrée.

4 boneless pork chops, cut to 1/2-inch thickness
1/2 teaspoon kosher salt
1/4 teaspoon coarsely ground black pepper
3 tablespoons clarified butter*, divided
1 1/2 cups thinly sliced white onion
2 1/2 cups cored and thinly sliced apples
3 tablespoons brown sugar, packed
1/2 teaspoon cayenne pepper
2 1/2 teaspoons ground cinnamon
1/3 cup apple cider
1/2 cup heavy cream
2 tablespoons pecans, toasted and chopped, for garnish

Preheat oven to 350 degrees. Coat a 2-quart baking dish with non-stick baking spray; set aside.
Toast pecans on a baking sheet in oven for 5-6 minutes until fragrant and brown; cool, chop and set aside.

Dry the pork chops thoroughly with a paper towel. Add salt and pepper to both sides of the chops.
In a large skillet, heat 2 tablespoons of clarified butter over high heat. When the butter is very hot and begins
to brown, add pork chops; sear both sides of the chops. Transfer browned chops to the baking dish.
Reheat skillet with remaining butter. Add sliced onions and apples; cook and stir over medium high heat
about five minutes or until onions and apples are tender. Mix in sugar, cayenne pepper, cinnamon, cider, and
cream. Spoon the onion and apple mixture over the pork chops.

Bake, uncovered, for 20 minutes. Turn oven heat off. Cover the baking dish with foil; allow to rest in the hot
oven for another 15 minutes. Transfer to serving plates; garnish with toasted pecans.

*Clarified butter has a high smoke point and is perfect to use with high heat. To clarify butter, melt 4
tablespoons solid butter in a small saucepan. Skim off the foam that appears on the top; discard. Pour off the
clear (clarified) yellow liquid into a dish to save, and discard milk solids left in the pan. (Four tablespoons
solid butter will equal about 3 tablespoons clarified butter.)

Rosemary Port Pork Roast

8 servings

An impressive and elegant dish to serve for dinner. The fragrance alone will get people to your table.

1 (about 4 pound) boneless, center cut pork roast
3 tablespoons good olive oil
4 teaspoons fresh rosemary, minced
3 cloves fresh garlic, minced
1/2 teaspoon kosher salt
1/2 teaspoon freshly ground black pepper
2 tablespoons Dijon mustard
2 tablespoons fresh lemon juice
Port Wine Sauce:
2 tablespoons good olive oil
1 1/2 tablespoons shallots, minced
1 1/2 teaspoons fresh rosemary, minced
1 teaspoon dried sage
2/3 cup dried cranberries
1 3/4 cup ruby port wine
1/3 cup beef broth
1/4 cup red wine vinegar
1/2 cup red currant jelly
1 1/2 tablespoons cornstarch mixed with 2 tablespoons cold water

Preheat oven to 400 degrees. Coat the bottom of a shallow roasting pan with non-stick cooking spray; set aside. Combine olive oil, rosemary, garlic, salt, pepper, mustard, and lemon juice to make a paste. Pat 3/4 of the mixture on the fat side of the roast; distribute remaining amount on the rest. Place fat side up in prepared pan. <u>Reduce oven temperature to 300 degrees: very important</u>. Roast, uncovered, for 2 hours or until a meat thermometer registers 145 to 150 degrees (begin checking at 1 hour, 45 minutes). Remove roast from oven; tent with foil and allow 15 minutes of rest time before slicing. Transfer meat to a platter or individual plates. Spoon warm sauce over slices and serve.

While pork is roasting, make sauce: Heat oil in a heavy skillet over medium heat. Add shallots, rosemary, sage, and cranberries. Cook and stir 2 minutes. Add wine, broth, vinegar, and jelly. Reduce heat to medium low; simmer 20 minutes, stirring frequently. Sauce will be reduced in volume and slightly thickened. Turn heat to medium. Bring sauce to a boil; stir in cornstarch mixture. Cook and stir until it is thick and smooth.

All American Meatloaf

Makes 2 loaves

Who doesn't like meatloaf? Here's your go-to recipe. You can serve one loaf tonight for dinner and save the other for sandwiches tomorrow.

2 pounds ground beef (80% lean, 20% fat)
1 pound ground pork (unseasoned)
3/4 cup onions, diced
3/4 cup celery, diced
3 cloves garlic, minced
2 eggs, beaten
1 15-ounce can tomato sauce
1/2 cup chili sauce
2 tablespoons Worcestershire
1 tablespoon Dijon mustard
1 tablespoon dried oregano
2 teaspoons kosher salt
1 1/2 teaspoons freshly ground black pepper
1/2 cup milk
2 tablespoons sour cream
2 cups fresh bread crumbs
1/2 cup fresh flat leaf parsley, minced

Preheat oven to 375 degrees. Using 2 forks (or your hands), lightly combine beef and pork in an extra large mixing bowl. Add onions, celery, garlic, eggs, tomato and chili sauces, Worcestershire, mustard, oregano, salt, and pepper; mix gently.

Whisk milk and sour cream together in a medium mixing bowl. Add bread crumbs and parsley; stir well. Combine crumb mixture with meat mixture, making sure all ingredients are evenly dispersed. Spoon into two 9 x 5 x 3-inch loaf pans. Bake 1 hour and 15 minutes. Remove from oven. Blot any accumulated fat from the top with a paper towel. Allow the meatloaves to rest 15 minutes before slicing to serve.

If you like a tomato-like topping, simply mix 1/4 cup ketchup, 1/4 cup chili sauce and 1 teaspoon Dijon mustard. Spread on top of each loaf before baking.

Date Night Beef Wellingtons

Photograph, page 104   *2 servings*

This is a special occasion dinner entrée that people will remember for a long, long time. I promise your effort and attention to detail will create a masterpiece.

2 (4-ounce) beef tenderloin filets
1 clove garlic, minced
1/4 teaspoon freshly grated lemon peel
1/2 teaspoon kosher salt
1/4 teaspoon freshly ground black pepper
1 tablespoon butter

Filling:
2 tablespoons dry sherry
4 ounces fresh mushrooms, finely chopped
2 tablespoons green onions, finely chopped
1 tablespoon fresh flat leaf parsley, finely chopped

Crust:
2 good quality frozen puff pastry shells, thawed
1 egg, beaten, and mixed with 1 tablespoon water

Wine Sauce:
1 tablespoon butter
2 tablespoons green onions, thinly sliced
3 fresh button or baby bella mushrooms, sliced
1 tablespoon all-purpose flour
1/4 cup dry red wine
2/3 cup beef broth
1 bay leaf
1/8 teaspoon kosher salt
1/8 teaspoon freshly ground black pepper
1/8 teaspoon Worcestershire sauce

- continued -

Wellingtons - Continued

Before you do anything else, make sure your pastry shells have thawed but are still cold. Keep in the refrigerator until you are ready to roll them out.

Preheat oven to 425 degrees. Place parchment on a baking sheet; coat lightly with non-stick cooking spray.

Mix garlic, lemon peel, salt, and pepper; rub on all surfaces of the beef. Heat butter in a small skillet (for best browning, do not use a non-stick skillet) on medium high heat. Add beef filets; cook 3 minutes on each side. Transfer to a paper towel lined plate; refrigerate. Add sherry to the pan drippings in the skillet; stir well. Add mushrooms, onions, and parsley; cook and stir 3 minutes until all liquid has evaporated. Set aside to cool.

Make wine sauce by melting butter over medium heat in a heavy saucepan. Add onions and mushrooms; cook and stir 3 minutes. Add flour, stirring to mix well. Stir in wine and broth; cook and stir until sauce thickens. Add bay leaf, salt, pepper, and Worcestershire. Reduce heat to low; simmer 10 minutes. Discard bay leaf. Set aside until filets have baked.

Roll out each pastry shell to a 6-inch round.

Spread equal portions of the cooled filling on top of each filet. Lay the pastry over the top; wrap it entirely. Turn it over; pinch all the edges of the pastry together to seal. Brush all surfaces with egg mixture; place filets on prepared baking sheet (seam side down). For a creative twist, place a flat leaf parsley sprig on top of the egg wash, seal it to the surface with another brush of egg wash. Sprinkle with a mixture of 1/8 teaspoon kosher salt and 1/8 teaspoon freshly ground black pepper - very pretty. Bake 15 minutes - crust will be golden in color. Remove from oven; allow to rest 10 minutes to redistribute juices.

Gently re-warm the wine sauce. Transfer filets to individual plates; serve with sauce on the side.

Shepherd's Pie

Photograph, page 107   *6 servings*

The Brits would call this Cottage Pie, as their Shepherd's Pie is made with ground lamb. I'll take artistic license, borrow the commonly-known name, and use beef instead.

1/4 cup butter
1 1/4 cups onions, finely diced
1 1/2 cup carrots, finely diced
3/4 cup celery, finely diced
2 large cloves fresh garlic, minced
1 1/2 pounds ground beef (85% lean)
1/4 cup all-purpose flour
2 tablespoons Worcestershire sauce
2 tablespoons tomato paste
1 cup dark beer (stout)
1 1/2 cups beef broth
1 tablespoon fresh rosemary
  (or 1 teaspoon dried), finely chopped
1 tablespoon fresh thyme
  (or 1 teaspoon dried), finely chopped

1 tablespoon flat leaf parsley, chopped
1 1/4 teaspoons kosher salt
3/4 teaspoon ground black pepper
1/4 teaspoon red pepper flakes
1 cup frozen peas
3 cups russet potatoes, cut in chunks
  (about 2 pounds)
4 tablespoons butter
1/3 cup heavy cream
2 egg yolks
1/2 cup grated Parmesan cheese,
  (divided)
1/4 teaspoon kosher salt
1/8 teaspoon ground black pepper

Preheat oven to 375 degrees. Lightly coat a 2-quart deep baking dish with non-stick cooking spray; set aside. Heat butter in a large skillet over medium heat. Add onions, carrots, and celery; cook and stir 6-8 minutes until vegetables are tender and lightly browned. Add garlic; cook 1 minute. Add beef; cook and stir vigorously until pieces are uniformly small and browned. Stir in flour; mix well. Add Worcestershire sauce, tomato paste, beer, and broth; cook and stir 3 minutes. Add rosemary, thyme, parsley, salt, pepper, and pepper flakes; mix well. Remove from heat; stir in peas. Spoon mixture into prepared dish; set aside.

Cook potatoes with enough cold water to cover and 1/2 teaspoon kosher salt until tender; drain. Mash cooked potatoes; add butter. Whisk cream and eggs together, add 1/4 cup Parmesan cheese, salt, and pepper: mix thoroughly with potatoes. Spoon mashed potato mixture over beef mixture. Top with remaining Parmesan cheese. Bake 25-30 minutes until heated through and top has browned. Serve hot.

Pheasant and Wild Rice

6-8 servings

What a lovely way to celebrate a fall harvest.

2 pheasants, using breast meat only
3/4 cups slivered almonds
1/2 cup all-purpose flour
1 teaspoon kosher salt
3/4 teaspoon black pepper
5 tablespoons butter, divided
8 ounces fresh mushrooms, sliced
1/4 cup red bell pepper, diced
1/4 cup green bell pepper, diced
2 medium cloves garlic, minced
3 cups cooked wild rice
1 1/2 cups chicken broth
1/2 cup dry white wine
1 cup heavy cream
1 teaspoon dried oregano, 1/2 teaspoon dried thyme
1/2 teaspoon kosher salt, 1/2 teaspoon black pepper

Preheat oven to 350 degrees. Place almonds in a single layer on a rimmed baking sheet. Bake 8-10 minutes until fragrant and edges are brown; set aside. Coat a 1 1/2- quart baking dish with non-stick cooking spray; set aside.

Cut pheasant into 1 1/2-inch cubes. Mix flour, salt, and pepper in a bowl; add pheasant pieces, and toss to coat well. Shake off extra flour; transfer pieces to a plate. Heat 3 tablespoons of butter in a large skillet over medium heat. Add pheasant; cook and stir 4 minutes until browned. Transfer pieces back to the plate. In the same pan, heat remaining 2 tablespoons butter. Add mushrooms, peppers, and garlic; cook and stir 2 minutes.

Add wild rice, broth, wine, cream, oregano, thyme, salt, pepper and reserved almonds; mix well. Simmer 10 minutes to blend flavors. Spoon into prepared baking dish; bake 45 minutes. Serve hot.

I doubt you will have any of this dish left over; however, in the rare case that you do, it may be reheated. Just add a little more broth or cream to rehydrate the rice.

Sauced Peppercorn Venison

4 servings

Classed-up venison steaks you will absolutely adore.

4 thick-cut venison steaks, trimmed of fat
1 tablespoon cracked black peppercorns
1 tablespoon cracked white peppercorns
1/2 teaspoon kosher salt
1 tablespoon good olive oil
Wine Sauce:
2 tablespoons butter
1/4 cup shallots, minced
4 large baby bella or button mushrooms, thinly sliced
2 medium cloves garlic, minced
1/2 cup dry white wine
2 tablespoons Dijon mustard
2/3 cup beef broth
2/3 cup heavy cream
1/2 teaspoon kosher salt
1/4 teaspoon freshly ground black pepper
3 tablespoons fresh flat leaf parsley, minced, and divided

Make sauce first. Melt butter in a small, heavy saucepan over medium heat. Add shallots and mushrooms; cook and stir 3 minutes until shallots are translucent. Add garlic and wine; cook about 4 minutes, or until mixture has been reduced by half. Whisk in mustard, broth, and cream. Season with salt and pepper. Cook about 15 minutes, stirring occasionally, until liquid has reduced in volume to about 1 cup. Stir in 2 tablespoons parsley. Set sauce aside; re-warm when the steaks are ready.

Mix black and white peppercorns; press into both sides of each steak. Season each side with salt. Heat oil over medium high heat in heavy skillet. When oil begins to shimmer, add steaks. Cook to desired doneness (actual time will be determined by the thickness of your steaks). Transfer steaks to a platter; tent with foil. Allow steaks to rest for 5 minutes before serving to allow redistribution of juices.

To serve, spoon sauce over the steaks; garnish with remaining parsley. Pairs well with mashed potatoes.

COOKING with MORE CONFIDENCE

Venison Swiss Steak

This will please even a wild game skeptic. Serve this with Creamy Mashed Potatoes (recipe, page 157) or Wild and Brown Rice Pilaf (recipe, page 95).

1 1/2 pounds venison steak
3/4 cup all-purpose flour
1 1/2 teaspoons kosher salt
1 teaspoon coarsely ground black pepper
1/8 teaspoon cayenne pepper
3 tablespoons butter, divided
1 tablespoon canola oil
1 1/2 cups onions, thinly sliced
1 14-ounce can diced tomatoes
1/2 cup red wine
1/2 teaspoon dried thyme
1/2 teaspoon dried marjoram
1/3 cup half and half
1 1/2 tablespoons fresh flat leaf parsley, minced

Mix flour with salt, black and cayenne peppers. Dredge steaks in the flour; shake off excess. Place each steak between 2 pieces of plastic wrap; pound out to about a 1/2-inch thickness, and dredge the second time in flour. Shake off excess flour; set aside.

Heat 2 tablespoons butter and oil in a large, heavy skillet over medium heat. Brown venison on both sides; transfer to a plate. Add remaining butter to the skillet; cook and stir onions 3-4 minutes until soft. Transfer onions to a plate.

Return steaks to the skillet. Cover the steak with cooked onions. Mix tomatoes with wine, thyme, and marjoram; spoon mixture over the steak and onions. Drizzle with cream. Reduce heat, and cover the skillet. Gently simmer for 15 minutes. Turn the steaks; continue to simmer 30 minutes until steaks are very tender. Check periodically - add a little more wine and/or cream if the sauce appears to be too thick.

Taste the sauce and adjust seasonings if necessary. Stir in parsley just before serving.

Scoops of Confidence

For Poultry, Meat, and Game

No roasting rack? No problem. Use celery ribs and carrots at the bottom of your roasting pan instead of a rack. A delicious answer.

To freeze bulk-purchased ground meat, divide portions and transfer meat to a zip-top bag. Remove air from the bag, and close. Flatten the package before freezing. The meat will defrost quickly and evenly.

A tablespoon of tomato paste added to tomato or brown sauces will deepen the color and brighten the flavor. Because tomato paste itself tastes rather harsh, allow your sauce to cook at least 2 more minutes to mellow flavors.

Salt does more to enhance and intensify flavors that any other ingredient or seasoning. If you are adding a coating of some kind to meat or chicken, think about drying it off first, adding salt and pepper, and then dredging with flour.

To achieve a perfect sear on steaks, chops, fish, or chicken, do not flip the pieces over until they release easily from the pan. Use tongs or spatula to turn instead of a fork.

Take meat to the grill on a foil-covered plate. Remove the foil, and you have a clean serving plate to take back to your table.

Allowing meat to rest before cooking relaxes its fibers and evaporates surface moisture for a more even sear. Rest time after cooking redistributes juices - 10 minutes for steaks and chops, 20 minutes for whole birds. Tent loosely with foil to keep warm during this process.

Placing frozen meat in a non-stick pan with a trace of water cuts your defrosting time in half.

Re-freezing meat is not a good idea. Liquid within the cells expands once it thaws and seeps out, causing the meat to lose its juices.

Reducing a sauce by half? Measure initial depth in your pan with a wooden skewer, and make a mark on it - easy to see progress when you re-check.

Allium cepa

(onion)

Sides

Asparagus Mushroom Pappardelle
Butternut Squash and Bacon
Overstuffed Tomatoes
Cauliflower Casserole
Confetti Sweet Corn
Pickled Red Onions
Caramelized Shallots
Sesame Stir Fry

Creamy Mashed Potatoes
Roasted Rosemary Garlic Potatoes
Roasted Parmesan Dill Potatoes
Scalloped Potatoes and Ham

Scoops of Confidence

Asparagus Mushroom Pappardelle

Such a nice, fresh taste to celebrate a late Spring day. This comes together quickly, so I would advise to prep the vegetables before you begin.

8 ounces lemon pappardelle* pasta
1 1/2 tablespoons butter
2 tablespoons good olive oil
2/3 cup onions, diced
2 cups fresh mushrooms, chopped
3 1/2 cups fresh asparagus – trimmed, and cut into 1-inch lengths
3/4 teaspoon kosher salt
1/2 teaspoon freshly ground black pepper
3/4 cup dry white wine
1 tablespoon freshly grated lemon peel
1/3 cup fresh lemon juice
2 1/2 cups fresh tomatoes, diced
2 tablespoons flat leaf parsley, finely chopped
1/2 cup freshly grated Parmesan cheese for garnish

Cook pasta according to directions on package. Drain; cover to keep warm.
Melt butter and oil together in a large skillet over medium heat. Add onions and mushrooms; cook and stir 2 minutes. Add asparagus pieces; cook and stir 1 minute. Season with salt and pepper. Transfer mushroom and asparagus mixture to a bowl; set aside.

Add wine, lemon peel, and lemon juice to the empty skillet; cook over medium heat to reduce by half in volume. Lower the heat. Stir in reserved mushroom and asparagus mixture, tomatoes, and cooked pasta; simmer 3-4 minutes until warmed through. Remove from heat, and stir in parsley. Transfer pasta to a serving bowl, and top with grated cheese.

Serve immediately.

*A substitute, if you do not have pappardelle, would be extra-wide and thicker egg noodles. If you do use regular noodles, add 1 extra teaspoon lemon peel to balance the flavors.

Butternut Squash and Bacon

A delectable side dish for your autumn table.   *4-6 servings*

1 3-pound butternut squash
6 slices bacon
3/4 cup chicken broth
3 tablespoons butter
1/2 teaspoon kosher salt
1/2 teaspoon freshly ground black pepper

Preheat oven to 400 degrees. Line a rimmed baking pan with foil; coat with non-stick spray; set aside. Cut squash in half lengthwise; use a spoon to remove seeds. Place (cut side down) on prepared pan; pierce skin in several places with a sharp knife to allow steam to escape while baking. Bake 40 minutes until soft and tender. Cut bacon crosswise into 1/4-inch strips. Place in a high-sided skillet or Dutch oven; cook and stir over medium heat until brown and crispy. Transfer pieces to a paper towel-lined plate to drain. To finish, scoop cooked squash from its peel - it should measure about 3 cups. Combine squash, broth, butter, salt, pepper, and bacon in the saucepan. When ready to serve, gently warm over medium low heat. Serve hot.

Overstuffed Tomatoes

When you want to round out a beautiful dinner plate, try this classic dish.   *4 servings*

4 medium tomatoes
1/2 teaspoon kosher salt, divided
1/2 teaspoon black pepper, divided
2 tablespoons butter
3/4 cup soft bread crumbs

2 tablespoons fresh parsley, minced
1 teaspoon dried oregano
1 clove garlic, minced
1/2 cup grated Parmesan cheese

Preheat oven to 400 degrees. Lightly coat a baking dish with butter; set aside.
Cut each of the tomatoes in half crosswise. Remove the seeds, and turn the halves face down on paper towels to drain. In a small skillet over medium heat, melt butter. Add bread crumbs, parsley, oregano, garlic, 1/4 teaspoon salt, and 1/4 teaspoon pepper. Toss until all the crumbs are coated and golden brown in color. Remove from heat; mix in cheese. Sprinkle remaining salt and pepper evenly inside each of the tomato halves. Fill tomatoes with bread crumb mixture. Place tomatoes in prepared baking dish; bake 20 minutes. Serve hot.

Cauliflower Casserole

Spoiler alert: There will be no leftovers. Combined cheeses impart a distinct flavor note and make an irresistible dish to pass around your family table.

7 cups cauliflower florets (from 1 large head)
4 strips thick bacon, diced to 1/2-inch pieces
3 tablespoons shallots, minced
2 tablespoons all-purpose flour
1 1/2 cups milk or half and half
1 teaspoon Dijon mustard
2/3 cup extra-sharp cheddar cheese, shredded
2/3 cup Gruyère cheese, shredded
1/4 cup blue cheese crumbles
2 ounces cream cheese, diced
1/2 teaspoon kosher salt
1/2 teaspoon freshly ground black pepper
1/2 teaspoon cayenne pepper
1/4 teaspoon freshly grated nutmeg
1/4 cup fresh parsley, minced and divided
3 tablespoons butter
1 1/2 cups fresh bread crumbs

Preheat oven to 375 degrees. Coat the inside of a 2-quart baking dish with non-stick cooking spray; set aside. Cook cauliflower in boiling, salted water for five minutes until tender-crisp. Transfer florets to paper towels to thoroughly drain and dry. Place bacon in a large saucepan over medium heat; cook and stir until crisp. Transfer pieces to paper towels, reserving bacon fat in the pan. Add shallots to the pan; cook and stir for 1-2 minutes until soft. Whisk in flour; cook and stir 1 minute. Add milk and mustard; whisk until smooth and thick.

Remove pan from heat. Add cheeses to the sauce; stir gently until completely melted. Stir in reserved bacon, cauliflower florets, salt, pepper, nutmeg, and 3 tablespoons parsley. Spoon mixture into prepared baking dish. Add butter to a small skillet; cook over low heat until lightly browned. Add bread crumbs; stir until coated with the browned butter. Distribute crumbs evenly on top of cauliflower mixture. Transfer casserole to the oven; bake 20 minutes. Change oven controls from Bake to Broil. Place casserole 6-8 inches below heating unit for 1-2 minutes until topping is golden brown. Allow dish to rest 10 minutes; garnish with remaining parsley. Serve hot.

Confetti Sweet Corn

6-8 servings

Whether at the peak of sweet corn season or in the dead of winter, this colorful combination of vegetables paired with the subtle flavor of bacon will brighten your table.

6 slices bacon, cut in 1/4-inch slices
3 tablespoons butter
2/3 cup onions, diced
2/3 cup celery, diced
4 cups corn kernels (cut fresh from the cob, or frozen)
1/2 cup orange bell pepper, diced
1/2 cup red bell pepper, diced
1/2 cup yellow bell pepper, diced
2 cloves garlic, minced
1 teaspoon freshly ground black pepper
1/2 teaspoon red pepper flakes
2 tablespoons fresh parsley, minced

Prepare onions, celery, peppers, garlic, and parsley as directed; set aside.

Place bacon slices in a large 4-quart skillet; cook and stir 5-7 minutes over medium heat until brown and crispy. Transfer cooked bacon to a plate; set aside.

Add butter to the bacon drippings in the skillet; stir to combine. Add onions and celery; cook and stir 3 minutes over medium heat; transfer to a bowl and set aside. Add corn; mix well, and cook 5 minutes over medium high heat. Stir only occasionally. As the corn cooks, some of its sugars will release - naturally resulting in a little charring and adding a layer of flavor.

Add peppers and garlic to the corn; cook and stir 2 minutes. Stir in reserved onions and celery, bacon pieces, red pepper flakes, black pepper, and parsley. Cook additional 2 minutes to blend flavors. Serve hot.

COOKING with MORE CONFIDENCE

Pickled Red Onions

Makes 2 cups

Tangy and tart, you will find pickled onions to be very versatile. Use them on a burger, salad, or sandwich for an extra punch of flavor. Terrific to have on hand, a staple in my refrigerator.

2 medium red onions, thinly sliced
2 cups white vinegar
3/4 cup granulated sugar
1/4 cup kosher salt
1 bay leaf
1 1/2 teaspoons peppercorns

Place onions in a glass bowl. Bring vinegar, sugar, salt, bay leaf, and peppercorns to a boil in a medium saucepan. Boil 1 minute. Pour boiling brine over onions. Cool to room temperature. Cover tightly, and refrigerate. They are the best quality if used within 3 to 4 weeks' time.

Caramelized Shallots

Makes 2 cups

A mild partner in the onion family, these shallots will top casseroles and/or potato dishes with flavor, crunch, and crispness.

2 cups shallots, thinly sliced
4 tablespoons butter

Heat 4 tablespoons butter in a large skillet over medium heat. Add shallots; cook and stir 10-12 minutes until shallots are caramel colored and tender. Transfer to a paper towel-lined plate; sprinkle with a little salt while still warm.

Sesame Stir Fry

Check your refrigerator. Chances are you will have all ingredients already on hand. Easily turn this into a vegetarian version by swapping out chicken broth for vegetable broth.

2 cups carrots, peeled and sliced
1 1/2 cups fresh broccoli florets
1 1/2 cups fresh cauliflower florets
1/3 cup walnuts, toasted and chopped
3 tablespoons vegetable oil
2 large cloves garlic, minced
1 tablespoon grated fresh ginger
2 cups fresh mushrooms, sliced
1 cup bell peppers, diced
1/2 teaspoon kosher salt

1/2 teaspoon ground black pepper
1/4 teaspoon red pepper flakes
4 tablespoons low-sodium soy sauce
1 teaspoon rice wine vinegar
1 teaspoon granulated sugar
1/2 cup chicken broth, divided
2 teaspoons cornstarch
1 tablespoon Asian sesame oil

Prepare all vegetables as directed; set aside. Bring 2 quarts water to a boil; add 1 tablespoon salt. Cook carrot slices for 2 minutes; transfer to ice water to stop the cooking. Add broccoli and cauliflower to boiling water and cook 1 minute; transfer to ice water. Remove all vegetables from ice water after a minute or so; transfer to paper towels to drain and dry.

In a large skillet over medium heat, cook and stir walnuts for about 1 minute until they are lightly toasted and fragrant; transfer to a dish and set aside. Heat oil in the skillet over medium heat. Add garlic and ginger; cook and stir 1 minute. Add mushrooms and peppers, along with the reserved carrots, broccoli and cauliflower; stir to thoroughly coat vegetables. Sprinkle with salt, pepper, and pepper flakes. Add soy sauce, vinegar, sugar, and 1/4 cup of the chicken broth. Cover the skillet; cook vegetables for about 3 minutes until tender-crisp.

Mix remaining 1/4 cup broth with cornstarch. Uncover the skillet; stir in sesame oil. Add cornstarch mixture; cook and stir 2 minutes until thickened. Toss vegetables gently with sauce.

Chop toasted walnuts. Transfer vegetables to a serving dish. Garnish with walnuts, and serve hot.

Creamy Mashed Potatoes

4-6 servings

Who wants to make mashed potatoes right before serving a big dinner? These can be made ahead of time; you will find the flavor and creamy texture to be so much better than the usual mash.

4 russet potatoes
4 tablespoons butter
1/4 cup onions, diced
2 cloves fresh garlic, minced
1/3 cup sour cream
1/4 cup whipping cream
1 1/4 cups extra-sharp cheddar cheese, shredded and divided
1 teaspoon fresh chives, thinly sliced
1/2 teaspoon kosher salt
1/4 teaspoon freshly ground black pepper
1 tablespoon fresh parsley, minced and divided

Preheat oven to 375 degrees. Coat a shallow 1-quart baking dish with non-stick cooking spray; set aside.

Peel potatoes and cut into even-sized chunks. Starting with cold water in a medium saucepan, add potatoes and a teaspoon of kosher salt; cook until soft enough to pierce easily with a knife. Drain and cover to keep warm.

Melt butter in a small skillet. Add onions; cook and stir 2 minutes. Add garlic; cook additional minute. Stir this mixture into hot, cooked potatoes; mash to desired consistency. Add sour cream, cream, 1 cup of the cheese, chives, salt, pepper, and 2 teaspoons of the parsley; mix well. Spoon potato mixture evenly into baking dish. Sprinkle with remaining cheese and parsley. Bake 20 minutes until potatoes are bubbly and slightly browned on top. Serve hot.

These potatoes can be made several hours in advance, covered, and refrigerated. To finish, bring dish to room temperature and bake as directed.

Roasted Potatoes

Guaranteed to please the potato lovers at your table, here are two flavor options...

<u>Rosemary Garlic Potatoes:</u> *8 servings*

2 pounds small red potatoes
1/2 cup butter, melted
4 cloves garlic, minced
1 teaspoon kosher salt
3/4 teaspoon freshly ground black pepper
1 teaspoon fresh rosemary, minced
2/3 cup grated Parmesan cheese, divided

Preheat oven to 425 degrees. Line a large, rimmed baking pan with foil; set aside.
Wash potatoes; cut into 3/8-inch slices. Rinse sliced potatoes in cold water to remove excess starch; dry thoroughly with paper towels. Combine butter, garlic, salt, pepper, rosemary, and 1/3 cup cheese in a large bowl. Add sliced potatoes; mix well. Arrange in a single layer on prepared pan; top with remaining cheese. Bake 20 minutes until potatoes are golden brown and slightly crisp. Serve hot.

<u>Parmesan Dill Potatoes:</u> *6 servings*

1 1/2 pounds small red potatoes
3 tablespoons good olive oil
3/4 teaspoon kosher salt
1/2 teaspoon freshly ground black pepper
2 tablespoons fresh parsley, minced
2 teaspoons dried dill weed
1/4 cup bread crumbs
1/2 cup grated Parmesan cheese

Preheat oven to 425 degrees. Line a large, rimmed baking pan with foil; set aside.
Wash potatoes; cut in 3/8-inch slices. Combine oil, salt, and pepper in a large bowl. Add sliced potatoes; toss gently to coat. Combine parsley, dill, bread crumbs, and cheese; add to oiled potatoes and mix well. Arrange in a single layer on prepared pan, making sure the crumb coating is evenly distributed on each potato slice. Bake 20-25 minutes until potatoes are tender and crisp. Serve hot.

COOKING with MORE CONFIDENCE

Scalloped Potatoes and Ham

Pure and simple, this is a shortcut version of a favorite comfort food. It will save you so much time when dinner has to be on the table in a hurry.

4 1/2 cups peeled red potatoes, sliced to a 3/8-inch thickness
2 cups whole milk
1 teaspoon kosher salt
1/3 cup onions, diced very small
1/2 cup cold water mixed with 2 tablespoons all-purpose flour
4 cups cooked ham, diced
2 tablespoons butter
1/2 teaspoon freshly ground black pepper
1 tablespoon fresh parsley, minced

Preheat oven to 375 degrees. Lightly coat a 2 1/2-quart baking dish with non-stick cooking spray; set aside. Place sliced potatoes in a 4-quart saucepan; add milk and salt. Over medium heat, bring potatoes to a boil. Reduce heat to medium low, and partially cover pan. Simmer potatoes for 12-15 minutes until they can be pierced easily with a fork. Add onions to cooked potatoes and milk. Stir in mixture of cold water and flour. Add ham, butter, pepper, and parsley; mix well.

Transfer potatoes to prepared dish. Bake 15-20 minutes until bubbly, and top is slightly browned. Remove from the oven, cover, and let stand for 10 minutes before serving.

This dish can be made ahead and gently reheated in a 300 degree oven.

Scoops of Confidence

For Sides

When making mashed potatoes, add butter first, and cream second. The butter coats the starch molecules in the potatoes, and prevents them from becoming "gummy" in texture.

Leftover Italian, French, or hearty country bread? Use a food processor to chop into crumbs, and freeze in zip top bags. Scoop out amount needed for your recipes.

The scoop on mushrooms:
Remove them from the store's plastic covered container and transfer to a paper bag - a regular lunch size is ideal. Fold over the top of the bag, and refrigerate. Storing them in this manner will increase their usable time threefold. When you're ready to use the mushrooms, simply clean and wipe with a damp paper towel.
Soaking dried mushrooms for a few hours in cold (not hot) water to rehydrate results in better flavor. Don't discard the water - it adds flavor in sauces or gravies.

Store fresh herbs by rolling them in a damp paper towel, and placing in a zip top freezer bag. Refrigerate. Quick way to mince fresh herbs? Use your pizza cutter.

Extra fresh garlic on hand? Mince it, and mix with just enough vegetable oil to coat. Freeze flat in a zip top bag 3-4 weeks without losing any of its flavor.

"Baby" carrots are cut from the root end of a regular carrot. Because they are already peeled, bagged, and stored, they naturally lose moisture and flavor. Freshly peeled carrots taste better and present better.

Canned beans are usually processed with a great deal of sodium. To reduce sodium content by nearly half, rinse beans under cold, running water for a minute or so, and proceed with your recipe.

Marking the bottoms of your baking dishes and casseroles with volume and size information eliminates guesswork when choosing the one you need.

Citrus limon

(lemon)

Sweets

Apricot Brandy Pound Cake
Banana Orange Cake
Blueberry Pound Cake
German Chocolate Cupcakes
Layered Carrot Cake
Lemon Cupcakes
Wicked Good Rhubarb Cake

Chocolate Coffee Cheesecake
Lemon Cheesecake

Double Coconut Cream Pie
Exceptional Apple Pie
Key Lime Island Pie

Cherry Berry Cobbler
Citrus Almond Mousse
Chocolate Espresso Pots de Crème
Chocolate Peanut Butter Tart
Coffee Ice Cream
Two Ways to Shortcake

Coconut Almond Chippers
Cranberry Crispers
Lemon Cream Double Deckers

Apple Cheesecake Bars
Cranberry Orange Bars
Rhubarb Custard Bars
Salted Turtle Squares
Scoops of Confidence

Apricot Brandy Pound Cake

Photograph, page 112   *16 servings*

Bake this a day ahead if you can. The taste intensifies when the flavors have an opportunity to blend.

1 cup butter, softened
3 cups granulated sugar
6 eggs
3 cups all-purpose flour
1/2 teaspoon kosher salt
1/4 teaspoon baking soda
1 cup sour cream
1 teaspoon pure vanilla extract
1 teaspoon pure lemon extract
1/2 teaspoon pure almond extract
1/2 teaspoon rum extract
1/2 cup apricot brandy
Glaze:
1 cup good quality apricot preserves
1 tablespoon apricot brandy
1 tablespoon heavy cream
1 1/2 cups confectioners' sugar
1/2 cup dried apricots, finely diced

Preheat oven to 325 degrees. Coat the inside of a 10-inch bundt pan generously with shortening. Lightly flour all the surfaces and shake out excess; set aside. (Do this even if you have a non-stick pan.) In a large bowl, beat butter and sugar until creamy. Add eggs, one at a time, beating after each addition. In a separate bowl, whisk flour, salt, and soda together. In a third bowl, combine sour cream, extracts, and brandy; mix well. Stir half the flour mixture and then half the sour cream mixture into the egg mixture. Repeat process with remaining flour and sour cream mixtures. Stir well. Spoon batter into prepared pan. Bake 80-90 minutes, until a wooden pick inserted near the center of the cake comes out clean. Remove from oven; cool 10 minutes on a wire rack. Invert cake, remove it from the pan; cool completely.

For glaze, mix preserves, brandy, and cream in a medium bowl. Add confectioners' sugar to obtain a good spreading consistency. Add a bit more cream or sugar if necessary. Frost top of cake, allowing glaze to drizzle down the sides. Sprinkle with apricot pieces.

Banana Orange Cake

Pure banana flavor with a boost of orange makes a lovely little cake.

1/2 cup butter, softened

3/4 cup granulated sugar

1/2 cup light brown sugar, packed

1 1/3 cups mashed bananas (about 3 medium)

2 eggs, beaten

1/2 cup sour cream

1 1/2 tablespoons frozen orange juice concentrate, thawed

1 teaspoon pure vanilla extract

2 teaspoons freshly grated orange peel

2 cups all-purpose flour

1 teaspoon baking soda

1/2 teaspoon kosher salt

Frosting:

4 ounces cream cheese, softened

4 tablespoons butter, softened

3/4 teaspoon pure vanilla extract

1 tablespoon frozen orange juice concentrate, thawed

3/4 teaspoon freshly grated orange peel

1 3/4 cups confectioners' sugar

Preheat oven to 350 degrees. Coat inside of a 9-inch round baking pan with non-stick cooking spray. Lightly dust with flour; set aside.

In a large bowl, combine butter and sugars; beat until thick and creamy. Add bananas, eggs, sour cream, orange juice concentrate, vanilla, and orange peel; mix well. Stir in flour, soda, and salt; mix gently until no traces of flour remain. Pour into prepared pan. Bake 50-55 minutes until top springs back when touched. Remove from oven; run a knife around the edge to separate cake from the pan. Cool 5 minutes; invert onto a wire rack to cool thoroughly.

For frosting, beat cream cheese, butter, vanilla, orange juice concentrate, and orange peel until smooth. Gradually add confectioners' sugar, beating until smooth and spreadable. Frost top of cooled cake. Cut in wedges to serve.

Blueberry Pound Cake

Fresh blueberries and orange come together nicely in this cake. Present it on your best pedestal plate.

1 tablespoon butter and 2 tablespoons granulated sugar for the baking pan
1 cup butter, softened
2 cups granulated sugar
4 eggs
1 tablespoon freshly grated orange peel
2 teaspoons frozen orange juice concentrate, thawed
1 teaspoon pure vanilla extract
3 cups all-purpose flour, divided
1/2 teaspoon kosher salt
1 teaspoon baking powder
2 cups fresh blueberries
Topping:
1 cup heavy cream
1 tablespoon confectioners' sugar
1 teaspoon pure vanilla extract

Preheat oven to 325 degrees. Butter a 10-inch tube (angel food) pan; evenly coat with sugar. Set aside.

In a large bowl, beat butter and sugar until creamy. Add eggs, one at a time, beating well after each addition. (Your batter should be light and fluffy.) Stir in orange peel, orange juice concentrate, and vanilla; blend well. Whisk 2 cups flour, salt, and baking powder together in a separate bowl. Add to egg mixture; beat well. Dredge blueberries in remaining 1 cup flour; stir to coat evenly*. Gently fold coated blueberries into creamed mixture. Spoon batter evenly into prepared pan. Bake 1 hour and 15 minutes until top springs back when touched, and toothpick inserted toward the center of the cake comes out clean. Transfer to a wire rack. After 5 minutes, run a knife around edges to loosen cake from the sides. Cool completely before removing from pan.

For the topping, whip cream with sugar and vanilla until soft peaks form. Slice cake; serve with whipped cream.

*This process will ensure berries will stay suspended in batter instead of sinking to the bottom of cake.

German Chocolate Cupcakes

16 cupcakes

Special dark cocoa adds richness and puts a new spin on this party perfect cupcake.

1/3 cup special dark Dutch processed cocoa

2 teaspoons instant espresso coffee powder

2/3 cup boiling water

2/3 cup buttermilk

2 teaspoons pure vanilla extract

3/4 cup butter, softened

1 1/2 cups granulated sugar

1/2 cup light brown sugar, packed

1/3 cup sour cream

3 eggs

2 cups all-purpose flour

1 teaspoon baking soda

3/4 teaspoon kosher salt

Cupcake Filling:

1 egg, well beaten

2/3 cup evaporated milk

2/3 cup granulated sugar

1/4 cup butter

1/2 teaspoon vanilla

1 2/3 cups sweetened flaked coconut

3/4 cup pecans, chopped

Frosting:

1 cup chocolate chips

1/2 cup butter, softened

2 tablespoons special dark cocoa

1 teaspoon vanilla

1/8 teaspoon kosher salt

2 1/2 cups confectioner's sugar

3 tablespoons milk, divided

8 slices bacon, cooked and crumbled

Preheat oven to 375 degrees. Coat muffin tins with non-stick cooking spray; set aside. Mix cocoa and espresso powder with boiling water; whisk well. Add buttermilk and vanilla; set aside. Beat butter until creamy. Add sugars; beat 3 minutes until light and fluffy. Beat in eggs, one at a time, until well blended. Add cocoa mixture and sour cream; stir well to combine. In a separate bowl, whisk together flour, soda, and salt. Fold flour mixture gently into the chocolate mixture. Fill prepared pans almost to the top. Bake 16-18 minutes (a toothpick inserted in the center of a cupcake should come out clean). Allow cupcakes to rest in the pans for 3-4 minutes; transfer to a wire rack to cool completely.

To make filling, cook and stir beaten egg, milk, sugar, and butter in a saucepan over medium low heat for 10 minutes until thick. Remove from heat; stir in vanilla, coconut, and pecans.

To make frosting, melt chocolate chips in a small saucepan over low heat. Remove from heat, stir in cocoa; mix well. In a deep bowl, beat butter until creamy. Add chocolate mixture, vanilla, 2 tablespoons milk, and salt; mix well. Beat in sugar gradually; add remaining milk and beat well to a spreadable consistency. To finish, cut each cupcake in half horizontally. Spoon filling on the bottom piece, and place the top half of cupcake over the filling. Frost cupcakes and garnish with bacon for a spectacular surprise finish.

Layered Carrot Cake

12 servings

A reliable recipe for a universally treasured and show-stopping cake. It stacks tall, looks majestic, and is a clear winner in the taste department.

4 eggs
1 1/2 cups granulated sugar
1 1/2 cups vegetable oil
2 cups all-purpose flour
2 teaspoons baking powder
2 teaspoons baking soda
1 teaspoon kosher salt
2 teaspoons ground cinnamon
1/4 teaspoon ground nutmeg
3 cups freshly grated carrots (about 6 medium-sized)
1/2 cup raisins, chopped
3/4 cup pecans, chopped
Frosting:
11 ounces cream cheese, room temperature
3/4 cup butter, room temperature
2 1/2 cups confectioners' sugar
1 20-ounce can crushed pineapple, well drained
1 tablespoon freshly grated lemon peel
1 1/2 teaspoons vanilla

Preheat oven to 350 degrees. Butter and flour 3 8-inch round baking pans; set aside. In a large bowl, beat eggs until frothy. Add sugar gradually; beat 3 minutes or until light and lemon colored. Slowly add oil, beating until well combined. In another bowl, whisk flour, baking powder, soda, salt, cinnamon, and nutmeg. Gently fold dry ingredients, a third at a time, into egg mixture. Add carrots, raisins, and pecans; stir well. Pour batter into prepared pans, taking care to even out quantities. Bake 30 minutes until top springs back when touched and a toothpick inserted in the center of each cake comes out clean. Cool completely. Using a serrated knife, carefully cut each layer in half horizontally. For the frosting, beat cream cheese and butter together until well combined. Add confectioners' sugar; beat until creamy. Stir in pineapple, lemon peel, and vanilla; mix well. Spread each layer with frosting, stacking them as you frost. Frost top and sides of cake. Chill at least 2 hours before slicing and serving.

Lemon Cupcakes

15 cupcakes

A frosted, melt-in-your-mouth treat with pure lemon flavor. Bet you can't eat just one…

<u>Cupcakes:</u>
4 eggs, separated
1 cup butter
1 cup granulated sugar
2 tablespoons freshly grated lemon peel
6 tablespoons fresh lemon juice
2 cups all-purpose flour
2 teaspoons baking powder
1/2 teaspoon kosher salt
<u>*Cream Cheese Lemon Frosting:*</u>
4 ounces cream cheese, room temperature
1/4 cup butter, room temperature
2 teaspoons freshly grated lemon peel
2 tablespoons fresh lemon juice
1 teaspoon pure vanilla extract
2 1/4 cups confectioners' sugar

Preheat oven to 375 degrees. Coat muffin tins with non-stick cooking spray; set aside.

Beat egg whites in a small, deep bowl until they reach stiff peaks; set aside. Beat egg yolks in another small, deep bowl until thick and lemon colored; set aside. In a medium bowl, combine butter and sugar; beat until light and fluffy. Add beaten egg yolks, lemon peel, and lemon juice; mix well. Whisk flour, baking powder and salt together; stir into egg and lemon mixture. Fold in reserved beaten egg whites; stir until just barely combined.

Fill muffin tins almost to the top.

Bake 15-17 minutes until edges have just started to brown and top springs back when touched. Cool completely.

For frosting, beat cream cheese and butter until thick and creamy. Add lemon peel, lemon juice, and vanilla; beat until smooth. With a small spatula, spread frosting on each cupcake.

COOKING with MORE CONFIDENCE

Wicked Good Rhubarb Cake

If you think rhubarb cake is ordinary fare, check this one out. Adding Vanilla Cream Topping when the cake is still warm from the oven changes it into a magical dessert.

Cake:

1 egg
1 cup buttermilk
1/3 cup butter, melted
1 teaspoon pure vanilla extract
3 cups rhubarb, finely chopped
1 cup granulated sugar
2 3/4 cup all-purpose flour
1 teaspoon baking soda
1/2 teaspoon kosher salt
1 cup light brown sugar, packed
3/4 cup walnuts, finely chopped

Vanilla Cream Topping:

1/2 cup butter, room temperature
1/2 cup heavy cream
1 cup granulated sugar
1 teaspoon pure vanilla extract

Preheat oven to 350 degrees. Butter and flour a 9 x 13 x 2-inch baking pan; set aside.

For the cake, mix egg, buttermilk, butter, and vanilla in a large bowl. Stir in rhubarb. In a separate bowl, combine sugar, flour, soda, and salt; add to the egg mixture; stir well. Spoon cake batter evenly into prepared pan. Combine brown sugar and walnuts; sprinkle mixture over the cake.

Bake 45 minutes, or until toothpick inserted in the center of the cake comes out clean.

For the Topping, combine butter, cream, and sugar in a small saucepan. Cook over medium heat until it comes to a boil. Remove from heat; add vanilla.

To finish, poke holes in the surface of the warm cake. Drizzle the warm sauce evenly over the cake. Cool completely. This cake may be served plain, or "fancied up" with a small dollop of sweetened whipped cream.

Chocolate Coffee Cheesecake

A glorious blend of chocolate and coffee makes this remarkable dessert sing with flavor.

<u>Crust:</u>

2 cups chocolate wafer crumbs

3 tablespoons granulated sugar

1/3 cup butter, melted

1/8 teaspoon kosher salt

<u>Filling:</u>

8 ounces bittersweet chocolate	**3 eggs**
2 tablespoons butter	**1/2 cup sour cream**
2 teaspoons instant espresso powder	**1/2 cup heavy cream**
2 teaspoons cocoa powder	**2 teaspoons pure vanilla extract**
2 8-ounce packages cream cheese	**2 cups fresh raspberries for garnish**
1 cup granulated sugar	
1/4 teaspoon kosher salt	

Preheat oven to 375 degrees.

For the crust, blend crumbs, sugar, butter, and salt. Press evenly into the bottom and about 1 inch up the sides of a 9-inch springform pan. Bake 10 minutes; transfer to a wire rack to cool. Reduce oven temperature to 325 degrees.

For the filling, chop chocolate; place in small saucepan along with better. Melt chocolate and butter over very low heat. Remove from heat; whisk in espresso powder and cocoa until smooth. Cool 5 minutes.

In a large bowl, beat cream cheese, sugar, and salt until smooth and creamy. Add eggs, one at a time, mixing well after each addition. Add cooled chocolate mixture; stir well. Whisk sour cream, heavy cream and vanilla together until smooth; gently fold into cream cheese mixture until no traces of cream are visible. Spoon filling into prepared crust. Bake 40-45 minutes until edges are set but center is still a bit jiggly. Turn off the heat; leave cheesecake in the oven (with the door closed) for 20 minutes. Remove cheesecake from the oven; transfer to a wire rack to cool completely. Cover with plastic wrap; refrigerate at least 3 hours. Remove sides from the pan. Slide a thin spatula under the crust to loosen it from the bottom of the pan; transfer to a flat serving plate.

To serve, cut in wedges; top with a few raspberries.

Lemon Cheesecake

Photograph, front cover, and page 98   *12 servings*

This is a no-bake cheesecake that always works and tastes better than divine.

Crust:
1 1/2 cups crushed vanilla wafers
6 tablespoons butter, melted
1 1/2 tablespoons granulated sugar

Filling:
3 tablespoons freshly grated lemon peel, divided
3/4 cup fresh lemon juice
1 tablespoon unflavored gelatin
1 1/4 cup granulated sugar
4 eggs + 2 egg yolks (save the whites in a separate bowl)
2 8-ounce packages cream cheese, room temperature
1/2 cup butter, room temperature
2 egg whites
1/8 teaspoon cream of tartar
3 tablespoons granulated sugar

Topping:
1 1/2 cups heavy whipping cream
2 teaspoons vanilla
2 tablespoons confectioners' sugar

Coat a 8-inch springform pan with pan spray. Mix crumbs, butter, and sugar; press into the bottom of prepared pan; set aside. For the filling, grate peel from 2 lemons; set aside. Measure lemon juice to total 3/4 cup. Add gelatin; stir to soften. In a medium saucepan, combine lemon mixture with sugar, eggs, and egg yolks; mix thoroughly. Cook and stir over low heat 3-4 minutes until thick (mixture should coat the back of a spoon). Remove from heat; stir in 2 tablespoons lemon peel, and set aside. In a large bowl, beat cream cheese and butter until smooth. Gradually add cooked lemon mixture to the cream cheese mixture; beat until smooth. Set aside to cool for 15 minutes. In a small, deep bowl, beat egg whites with cream of tartar until soft peaks form. Add sugar gradually, beating until stiff peaks form. Gently fold egg white mixture into the cooked and cooled lemon mixture. Spoon into prepared crust; refrigerate at least two hours.

For the topping, beat cream, vanilla, and confectioners' sugar until soft peaks form; spread on top of cooled cheesecake. Garnish with remaining lemon peel.

Double Coconut Cream Pie

No artificial flavors here - just homemade pie with real coconut that tastes worlds better than one you could buy.

2/3 cup granulated sugar
1/4 cup cornstarch
1/4 teaspoon kosher salt
2 cups whole milk
3 egg yolks, lightly beaten
2 tablespoons butter
1 teaspoon pure vanilla extract
3/4 cup shredded, sweetened coconut
1 9-inch pie crust*, baked
Meringue:
3 egg whites
1/4 teaspoon cream of tartar
1/3 cup granulated sugar
1/2 cup shredded, sweetened coconut

Preheat oven to 350 degrees.

Whisk sugar, cornstarch, and salt together in a medium saucepan. Add milk; whisk until well blended. Cook over medium low heat, stirring constantly, until mixture thickens and comes to a boil. Remove from heat. Gradually add about a cup of the hot mixture to the egg yolks; whisk well to combine. Stir this mixture back into remaining hot mixture. Return to heat. Cook 2 more minutes, stirring constantly. Add butter and vanilla; mix until well blended. Stir in coconut. Cool 10 minutes before spooning into your baked pie crust. For the meringue, beat egg whites with cream of tartar until foamy. Gradually add sugar, beating until stiff peaks form. Spread meringue over pie, making sure it extends all the way out to touch pie crust. Sprinkle coconut evenly over meringue. Bake 10-12 minutes until meringue has turned light brown in color.

Chill at least 2 hours before slicing and serving.

If you are in a hurry and don't have time to make pie, you can certainly use this recipe as a dessert. Simply chill the filling, and spoon into individual dishes. Top with sweetened whipped cream and coconut.

*Pie Pastry (recipe, page 56)

Exceptional Apple Pie

6 servings

Definitely worth the effort, with blue ribbon results.

Crust:

3 cups all-purpose flour
1 tablespoon dark brown sugar
1 teaspoon kosher salt
1/2 cup butter-flavored shortening, chilled and cut in small pieces
1/2 cup unsalted butter, chilled and cut in small pieces
1/2 cup ice cold water
1 egg yolk + 1 teaspoon water

Whisk flour, sugar, and salt together. Add shortening and butter. Using a pastry blender or food processor, combine until mixture resembles coarse meal. Slowly add water to make a soft dough. Cover with plastic wrap and refrigerate for 20 minutes. Lightly coat a 9-inch glass pie plate with non-stick cooking spray. Divide chilled pastry in half. Roll out the first half to a 12-inch circle. Place in prepared dish; leave about 3/4-inch extra pastry all around. Whisk egg yolk and water together; brush mixture on bottom and sides of crust (keeps pastry from becoming soggy). Refrigerate 10 minutes while making pie filling.

Filling:

6 cups (about 2 pounds) Granny Smith apples, cored, peeled, and thinly sliced
2 tablespoons fresh lemon juice
2/3 cup granulated sugar and 1/2 cup dark brown sugar
1/2 cup all-purpose flour
1 teaspoon cinnamon
1/8 teaspoon nutmeg
1/8 teaspoon allspice
1 egg, beaten
1 1/2 tablespoons bourbon
2 tablespoons butter, cut in small pieces

Preheat oven to 425 degrees. Combine apples, juice, sugars, flour, spices, egg, and bourbon in a large bowl; mix well. Mound filling into pie shell. Top with butter pieces. Roll out remaining half of pastry; cover your filling. Crimp edges, and make several piercings in the top crust for air to escape during baking. Bake 10 minutes. Reduce heat to 350 degrees. Bake 50-55 minutes until apples are tender and top is nicely browned. Cool at least 30 minutes (allowing filling to set) before serving.

Key Lime Island Pie

If you need a dose of sweet summertime goodness or a reminder of a warm ocean breeze, treat yourself to this pie. It will transport you to a happy place.

Crust:

1 1/4 cup graham cracker crumbs
1/4 cup granulated sugar
1/3 butter, melted

Filling:

1 1/2 cups granulated sugar
1 1/2 cups water
6 tablespoons cornstarch
1 tablespoon freshly grated lime peel
1/2 cup lime juice*
2 ounces coconut rum (optional)
3 egg yolks, slightly beaten

Preheat oven to 375 degrees.

For the crust combine crumbs, sugar, and butter. Pat into 9-inch pie plate. Bake for 8-10 minutes until lightly browned. Remove from oven; cool completely.

For filling, bring sugar and water to a boil in a heavy saucepan. Combine cornstarch, lime peel, and juice in a small bowl. Add egg yolks; stir to blend well. Add about a cup of the hot sugar water to egg mixture; stir well to warm. Whisk blended egg mixture into remaining hot sugar water. Stir until mixture comes back to a boil. Remove from heat; add coconut rum. Cool 15 minutes; pour into prepared pie crust.

Top with sweetened whipped cream.

Should you decide to use bottled Key lime juice for the pie filling, consider purchasing at least one fresh lime for the grated peel. It makes a big fresh flavor difference.

*Use the juice of 5 Persian (common) limes or a good quality bottled Key lime juice.

Cherry Berry Cobbler

Photograph, page 106   *8 servings*

Made with frozen berries and packed with intense flavors, this is picture-perfect for your table anytime of year.

Berry Filling:

1 10-ounce package frozen raspberries, thawed
1 10-ounce package frozen blackberries, thawed
1 10-ounce package frozen sweet cherries, thawed
2 teaspoons freshly grated lemon peel
3 tablespoons Kirsch (cherry brandy) or orange juice
1 cup granulated sugar
1/2 cup water
1/2 cup cornstarch
1 cup fresh blueberries

Cobbler Topping:

1 1/2 cups all-purpose flour
1 1/2 tablespoons granulated sugar
2 1/4 teaspoons baking powder
3/4 teaspoon cinnamon
6 tablespoons butter
3/4 cup heavy cream
1 tablespoon coarse sanding sugar

Preheat oven to 425 degrees. Coat a 2-quart casserole with non-stick cooking spray; set aside. In a large saucepan, combine raspberries, blackberries, cherries, lemon peel, and cherry brandy. Stir in sugar.

Mix water and cornstarch together; add to berry mixture. Bring to a simmer over medium heat. Cook and stir about 3-4 minutes until sauce is shiny and thick; remove from heat. Stir in blueberries. Spoon mixture into prepared dish.

For the cobbler topping, whisk flour, sugar, baking powder, and cinnamon together in a medium bowl. Add butter; mix with a pastry blender or a fork until it resembles coarse crumbs. Add cream; mix lightly with a fork until just blended. Drop batter by small spoonfuls on top of berry mixture, covering entire surface. Sprinkle top evenly with sanding sugar. Bake 25 minutes until cobbler topping is brown and toothpick inserted in center of topping comes out clean. Cool 10-15 minutes. Serve warm. If made ahead, rewarm in 325 degree oven.

Citrus Almond Mousse

4 generous servings

A light and luscious dessert to celebrate a wonderful meal. The fresh citrus medley makes it a special tangy treat.

1/2 cup sliced almonds, toasted
1 tablespoon unflavored gelatin
1/4 cup cold water
1 cup granulated sugar
1/2 cup water
3 tablespoons freshly grated orange peel
1 tablespoon freshly grated lemon peel
1 1/4 cups fresh orange juice
2 tablespoons fresh lemon juice
1 cup heavy cream

Preheat oven to 350 degrees. Place almonds in one layer on a baking sheet. Bake 5-6 minutes until fragrant and light brown in color. Remove from oven; set aside to cool.

Stir gelatin into 1/4 cup cold water; set aside for 5 minutes.

Combine sugar, 1/2 cup water, orange and lemon grated peel in a small saucepan. Heat to boiling; boil for 1 minute. Remove from heat; add softened gelatin into mixture; stir until gelatin has dissolved. Add orange and lemon juices; mix well. Transfer warm mixture to a bowl; refrigerate until slightly thickened.

Whip cream until soft peaks have formed. Stir about 1/4 of the whipped cream into the thickened fruit juice mixture; mix well. Fold in remaining whipped cream until well blended. Divide dessert into glass dishes (use stemmed goblets if you have them). Garnish with toasted almonds. Refrigerate until ready to serve.

COOKING WITH MORE CONFIDENCE

Chocolate Espresso Pots de Crème

6 generous servings

Exceptional taste and presentation make this decadent, do-ahead dessert well worth the prep.

6 ounces fine-quality bittersweet (not unsweetened) chocolate, finely chopped
1 1/3 cups heavy whipping cream
2/3 cup whole milk
1 1/2 teaspoons instant espresso powder
1/8 teaspoon kosher salt, divided
6 large egg yolks
2 tablespoons granulated sugar
Topping:
1 cup heavy cream, whipped
2 tablespoons confectioners' sugar
1 teaspoon pure vanilla extract
6 ounces fresh raspberries (or chocolate curls) for garnish

Place oven rack in the middle position, and preheat oven to 300 degrees. Line a 9 x 13-inch baking pan with a thin, folded kitchen towel. Arrange six 4 to 5-inch ramekins on towel. Poke several holes in a large sheet of foil with a skewer; set aside.

Place chopped chocolate in a heatproof bowl; set aside.

In a medium-sized heavy saucepan, bring cream, milk, espresso powder, and half of the salt just to a boil, stirring until espresso powder is dissolved. Pour heated mixture over chocolate, whisking until chocolate is melted and mixture is smooth.

In another bowl, whisk together egg yolks, sugar, and remaining salt. Add warm chocolate mixture in a slow stream, whisking constantly. Pour custard through a fine-mesh sieve into a 4-cup glass measure and cool, stirring occasionally, about 15 minutes. Skim off any foam that may appear on top.
Divide the custard evenly into ramekins in prepared pan. Create a hot water bath by adding VERY hot water around the ramekins in the baking pan until water comes halfway up ramekins' sides (take care not to splash water into the custards). Cover the pan tightly with prepared foil. Bake until custards are set around edges but still a bit wobbly in centers, 30 to 35 minutes. Remove from oven, and transfer ramekins carefully to a rack to cool completely (about 1 hour). Custards will set as they cool.

Cover each ramekin with plastic wrap; chill about 3 hours. Garnish with sweetened whipped cream and berries (or chocolate curls).

Chocolate Peanut Butter Tart

8 servings

When you need a dessert that kids of all ages will love, choose this one. You may want to hide it in the very back of the refrigerator so it doesn't mysteriously disappear at midnight.

Crust:
1 3/4 cups chocolate sandwich cookie crumbs (about 18 cookies)
5 tablespoons butter, melted
1/3 cup dry roasted peanuts, finely chopped

Filling:
1 1/4 cups heavy cream
1/2 cup confectioners' sugar
1 1/2 teaspoons pure vanilla extract
1 8-ounce package cream cheese, room temperature
1 cup creamy peanut butter, room temperature

Topping:
1/4 cup heavy cream
1/2 cup semi-sweet chocolate chips

Preheat oven to 325 degrees. Coat the inside of a 9-inch tart pan (with a removable bottom) with non-stick cooking spray. For stability purposes, set the pan on a rimmed baking sheet. Using a small food processor, grind cookies into smooth crumbs (or you can use a rolling pin to crush the cookies between two layers of waxed paper). Mix cookie crumbs with melted butter. Pat mixture in the bottom and up the sides of the tart pan. Sprinkle evenly with chopped peanuts; press them firmly into the cookie crust. Bake 15 minutes. As soon as it comes out of the oven, use the back of a spoon to pat the edges and bottom of the crust firmly in place; cool completely.

In a narrow, deep bowl, whip cream, sugar, and vanilla until soft peaks form; set aside. Combine cream cheese and peanut butter in another bowl; beat until smooth and creamy. Add half the whipped cream mixture; stir until thoroughly mixed. Gently fold in remaining whipped cream, blending until mixture is smooth and no trace of the cream remains. Spoon filling into cooled crust, making sure it touches the edges. Use a spatula if necessary to smooth top to an even level.

For the topping, gently warm cream in a small saucepan. Add chocolate chips; stir until smooth and glossy. Cool to room temperature. Drizzle decoratively over top of the tart. Refrigerate for at least 2 hours. Remove edges from the tart pan. Loosen the tart from the pan bottom; transfer to a serving plate. Cut in wedges and serve cold.

COOKING WITH MORE CONFIDENCE

Coffee Ice Cream

Makes 1 quart

This ice cream far surpasses any coffee-flavored you can buy. It's well worth the time to make your own.

1 cup coffee beans, medium roast
2 cups heavy cream
1 cup whole milk
3/4 cup granulated sugar
1/8 teaspoon kosher salt
2 teaspoons instant espresso powder
5 egg yolks
1 teaspoon pure vanilla extract

Place coffee beans in a sturdy zip top bag. Using a rolling pin or other heavy device, crush the beans; set aside.

Mix cream, milk, sugar, and salt in a medium saucepan. Warm over medium heat, stirring occasionally, until sugar dissolves and bubbles begin to form at the edges of the pan. Remove from the heat. Add crushed coffee beans, cover the pan tightly, and let the beans steep for about an hour to impart flavor.

Pour coffee flavored mixture through a fine mesh strainer into a bowl; discard beans. Add espresso powder; whisk well to combine.

In a separate bowl, beat egg yolks until thick and creamy. Gradually add the flavored milk mixture into the egg yolks; whisk well. Return this mixture back to the saucepan. Cook over low heat, stirring constantly, until it thickens slightly and coats the back of your spoon. Do not boil.

Strain cooked custard into a bowl to remove any lumps that may have formed. Stir in vanilla. Cover the bowl with plastic wrap and refrigerate for 20-30 minutes. Pour into ice cream maker, and process according to manufacturer's directions. Spoon finished ice cream into a container, cover, and place in your freezer for at least two hours until firm.

Two Ways to Shortcake

6 servings

A popular dessert, with two of my favorite fruit options that make these tall in the taste department.

2 cups all-purpose flour

2 teaspoons baking powder and 1/2 teaspoon baking soda

3/4 teaspoon kosher salt

2 tablespoons granulated sugar

4 tablespoons butter, chilled and cut in small pieces

3 tablespoons shortening

2/3 cup buttermilk mixed with 1/2 teaspoon pure vanilla extract

1 teaspoon cream and 1 teaspoon coarse sanding sugar for topping

Preheat oven to 425 degrees. Whisk flour, baking powder, soda, salt, and sugar together in a bowl. Using a pastry blender (or your hands), cut butter and shortening into the flour mixture until it resembles coarse crumbs. Mix buttermilk and vanilla together. Slowly add this the flour mixture, combining gently with a fork until it turns into a soft dough. Turn the dough out on a lightly floured surface; roll to a 1/2-inch thickness. Cut 3-inch circles or squares; place on an ungreased baking pan about 1 inch apart. Brush tops with cream and sprinkle with sugar. Bake 15-18 minutes until bottoms are browned and tops are firm to the touch. Allow to rest 10 minutes before splitting in half.

Strawberry:

4 cups fresh strawberries, hulled

2 tablespoons granulated sugar

Mash about 1/3 of the berries into small chunks. Slice remaining berries 1/4-inch thick. Mix the sliced and mashed berries together; add sugar, and let stand at room temperature 30 minutes. Spoon berries on split shortcakes. Top with ***Sweetened Whipped Cream***: beat 1 1/2 cups cold whipping cream with 2 tablespoons confectioners' sugar and 1 teaspoon pure vanilla extract until soft peaks form.

Peach:

4 peaches

1/2 cup light brown sugar, packed

1/4 cup water

1 tablespoon amaretto (or peach schnapps)

Mix brown sugar and water in a small saucepan; bring to a boil over medium heat. Remove from heat; set aside to cool. Easy-peel peaches by dropping them into boiling water for 1 minute, then plunging into ice water. Peel each peach, cut in half and remove pit. Cut into 1/2-inch slices, and place in bowl. Mix amaretto or peach schnapps into cooled sugar water; add to peaches; cover, and refrigerate 30 minutes to blend flavors. Spoon peaches on split shortcakes; top with sweetened whipped cream (recipe, above).

Coconut Almond Chippers

Crunchy cookies that are packed with flavor. Serve them on that pretty plate you received from Grandma.

1/4 cup butter, softened
1/4 cup vegetable shortening
3/4 cup granulated sugar
3/4 cup light brown sugar, packed
2 eggs, lightly beaten
1 1/2 teaspoons pure vanilla extract
2 1/4 cups all-purpose flour
1 teaspoon baking soda
3/4 teaspoon kosher salt
2 cups semi-sweet chocolate chips
1 cup sweetened coconut
1 cup slivered almonds, toasted*, and coarsely chopped

Preheat oven to 350 degrees.

*Toast almonds by placing them on a dry baking sheet. Bake 8-10 minutes until lightly browned and fragrant. Remove from oven; cool, and chop. Set aside.

Increase oven temperature to 375 degrees. Line baking sheets with parchment; set aside.

Combine butter, shortening, and sugars in a large bowl; beat until creamy. Beat in eggs and vanilla. Stir in flour, baking soda, and salt; mix well. Add chips, coconut, and almonds; mix well. Form into 1 1/2-inch balls, place on baking sheet, and flatten.

Bake 8-10 minutes; transfer to a rack to cool completely.

These cookies freeze beautifully.

Frosted Cranberry Crispers

Makes about 2 1/2 dozen

A favorite cookie because of its texture and taste. This recipe can easily be doubled for a crowd.

1/2 cup butter, softened
1/4 cup vegetable shortening
1/2 cup light brown sugar, packed
1/4 cup granulated sugar
1 egg
1 1/2 teaspoons pure vanilla extract
3/4 cup dried cranberries (or dried cherries), chopped
3/4 cup old-fashioned rolled oats
3/4 cup walnuts, finely chopped
1 1/2 cups all-purpose flour
1/2 teaspoon baking powder
1/2 teaspoon baking soda
1/4 teaspoon kosher salt
Frosting Drizzle:
1/2 cup confectioners' sugar
3 tablespoons milk or cream
1/4 teaspoon pure vanilla extract

Preheat oven to 350 degrees. Line baking sheets with parchment paper; set aside.

Mix butter, shortening, and sugars in a medium bowl. Add egg and vanilla; beat until batter is light in color. Add cranberries, oats, and walnuts; stir well to distribute evenly. In a separate bowl, mix flour, baking powder, soda, and salt; stir into the cranberry mixture.

Roll dough into 1 1/2-inch balls; place on baking sheet, and flatten slightly. Bake 15-18 minutes until cookies are light brown in color and slightly firm to the touch. Transfer to a rack to cool completely. For frosting, mix sugar, milk, and vanilla. With cookies resting on the cooling rack, drizzle a scant 1/2 teaspoon of frosting in a crisscross design on top of each.

Before storing or freezing, make sure the frosting is completely set and dry.

Lemon Cream Double Deckers

Photograph, page 105   *Makes 40 sandwich cookies*
With the purest taste of lemon and cream cheese filling, these fancy cookies will disappear quickly.

Lemon-Infused Flavoring:
2 1/2 teaspoons freshly grated lemon peel
1/4 cup fresh lemon juice

Cookies:
1 cup butter, room temperature
1 1/2 cups granulated sugar
2 eggs
2 tablespoons reserved lemon-infused flavoring
1 tablespoon freshly grated lemon peel
1/2 teaspoon pure lemon extract
3 cups all-purpose flour
1/2 teaspoon kosher salt
1/2 teaspoon baking soda

Filling:
1 8-ounce package cream cheese
2 tablespoons freshly grated lemon peel
2 1/2 cups confectioners' sugar

Preheat oven to 350 degrees. Line baking sheets with parchment; set aside.

For the flavoring, combine lemon peel and juice in a small saucepan over medium heat. Bring mixture to a boil; reduce heat, and continue to simmer for 6-8 minutes until it has reduced to about 2 tablespoons. Remove from heat; cool, and save to include in cookie dough.

For the cookies, combine butter and sugar in a large bowl; beat until thick and creamy. Add eggs, reserved lemon-infused flavoring, lemon peel, and extract; beat until smooth. Add flour, salt, and baking soda; mix to soft dough. Roll into small 1-inch balls; chill for 15 minutes. Place on baking sheet and flatten slightly, making sure each cookie will be nice and round. Bake 15 minutes until the cookie edges have just started to brown; transfer to a rack to cool completely.

For filling, mix cream cheese, lemon peel, and confectioners' sugar until thick and smooth.
To assemble, spread the bottom of one cookie with filling and place the bottom side of another cookie on top. Press together so filling protrudes outside of the cookie edges just a little. Store, refrigerated, in an airtight container.

Apple Cheesecake Bars

Photograph, page 103   *Makes about 20 servings*

A combination of apple pie and cheesecake for a four-layered treat.

First Layer (crust):

2 cups all-purpose flour

1/2 cup light brown sugar, packed

1 cup butter, room temperature

1/2 teaspoon ground cinnamon

1/4 teaspoon ground nutmeg

Second Layer (cream cheese filling):

3 (8-ounce) packages cream cheese, room temperature

3 eggs

1 1/2 teaspoons pure vanilla extract

Third Layer (apples):

4 1/2 cups Granny Smith apples, cored, peeled, and finely chopped

3 tablespoons granulated sugar

1/2 teaspoon ground cinnamon

1/4 teaspoon ground nutmeg

1/4 teaspoon kosher salt

1/2 cup water

Fourth Layer (streusel topping):

1 cup light brown sugar, packed

1 cup all-purpose flour

1/2 cup old-fashioned rolled oats

1/2 cup butter

1/2 cup caramel sauce, optional

Preheat oven to 350 degrees. Lightly coat a 9 x 13-inch pan with cooking spray; set aside. Using a pastry blender (or your hands), combine all crust ingredients; pat evenly into the bottom of prepared pan. Bake 15 minutes; cool. In a medium bowl, whip cream cheese until smooth. Add eggs, one at a time; mix until well blended. Stir in vanilla. Spread this mixture over the baked, cooled crust. Combine chopped apples, sugar, cinnamon, nutmeg, salt, and water in a medium saucepan. Bring mixture to a boil; reduce heat, cover, and simmer 10 minutes. Lightly mash to resemble chunky applesauce; cool. Spoon evenly over the cream cheese layer. Combine streusel topping ingredients; sprinkle over the apple layer. Bake 50 minutes until the filling has set and topping has browned. Cool. Cut in squares. If you desire, serve with a drizzle of caramel sauce.

Cranberry Orange Bars

Makes about 20 servings

A surprising sweet-tart flavor combination you will love.

Bars:
1/2 cup butter, room temperature
1 1/2 cups granulated sugar
2 eggs
1 1/2 tablespoons orange juice concentrate, thawed
1 teaspoon pure vanilla extract
1 1/2 cups all purpose flour
1/2 teaspoon kosher salt
1 teaspoon baking powder
1/2 cup pecans, finely chopped
2 1/2 cups fresh cranberries

Orange Glaze:
2 cups confectioners' sugar
3 tablespoons milk or cream
3 tablespoons orange juice concentrate, thawed
1 teaspoon pure vanilla extract

Preheat oven to 350 degrees. Grease and flour a 9 x 13 x 2-inch baking pan; set aside.

In a medium-sized bowl, combine butter and sugar; beat until light and fluffy. Add eggs, orange juice concentrate, and vanilla; blend well. Add flour, salt, and baking powder; mix well (your batter will be very thick). Stir in pecans. Spoon batter into prepared pan. Distribute cranberries evenly over surface of the batter. Using your hands (or a flat spatula) press the cranberries firmly into the batter.

Bake 35 to 40 minutes until top has browned and sides start to pull away from the pan. Cool 10 minutes. For the glaze, mix all ingredients to a very smooth consistency. Pour evenly over top of the bars, and cool completely. Cut into squares to serve.

Rhubarb Custard Bars

Makes about 20 servings

A rhubarb delight for mid-morning, mid-afternoon, or midnight.

2 2/3 cups all-purpose flour, divided
3/4 cup confectioners' sugar
1 cup butter, room temperature
4 eggs
1 3/4 cup granulated sugar
1 teaspoon kosher salt
4 1/2 cups rhubarb, diced*

Preheat oven to 350 degrees.

Butter a 9 x 13 x 2-inch baking pan; set aside.

Mix 2 cups of the flour, confectioners' sugar, and softened butter until it comes together as a smooth, soft dough. Pat evenly into bottom of prepared pan. Bake 18 minutes.

Beat eggs and granulated sugar together until thick, smooth, and lemon-colored. Add remaining 2/3 cup flour and salt; mix to form a thin batter. Add rhubarb, stirring well to distribute evenly. Spoon rhubarb mixture over baked crust. Return the pan to the oven; bake additional 45-50 minutes until the top is just turning brown at the edges, and is firm to the touch.

Using a hot, dry knife, cut bars while still a bit warm. Serve cool or at room temperature.

*Frozen rhubarb may be used. You will want to thaw the pieces first on a paper towel so any ice crystals are melted and absorbed. If using frozen rhubarb, allow about an extra cup to make up for moisture and volume lost in the freezing process.

Salted Turtle Squares

An impressive treat for the sweet and salty.

1 1/4 cups butter, divided
1 2/3 cups light brown sugar, packed and divided
2 cups all-purpose flour
1 1/2 cups pecans, roughly chopped
1 cup semi-sweet chocolate chips
1 teaspoon coarse sea salt for finishing

Preheat oven to 350 degrees. Coat a 9 x 13-inch baking pan with non-stick cooking spray; set aside.

Mix 1/2 cup butter, 1 cup brown sugar, and flour in a medium bowl until a dense, crumb-like texture is achieved. Pat evenly into the bottom of prepared pan. Sprinkle pecans evenly over the first layer; press firmly.

Bake 12 minutes; remove from oven.

Combine 3/4 cup butter and 2/3 cup brown sugar in a small saucepan. Cook over medium heat, stirring constantly, until mixture comes to a boil. Reduce heat to low, continue stirring; cook additional 3 minutes. Remove from heat, and pour evenly over the baked crust. Return pan to the oven; bake 15 minutes. Remove pan from the oven. Distribute chocolate chips evenly on top. Wait 2 minutes until chips begin to melt. With a large spoon or offset spatula, spread chocolate evenly.

Sprinkle with sea salt. Cool completely before cutting bars with a sharp knife.

Scoops of Confidence

For Sweets

By law, pure vanilla extract has to contain 35% alcohol. If it contains less, it has to be called vanilla flavoring. I say use the good stuff, and leave the imitations at the store. Pure vanilla extract is well worth the cost.

Vegetable shortening adds structure, and butter adds flavor to your cookies. If you're using all butter, chilling the cookies before baking will help retain their shape.

Sweetened condensed milk, because of its high sugar content, cannot be used in place of evaporated milk in a recipe. Evaporated milk, however, can be used as a substitute for regular milk in recipes if it is mixed with an equal amount of water.

Avoid chocolate "seizing" (becoming lumpy and grainy) by melting it over very low heat. This is especially necessary when melting chocolate chips, because they contain oil additives to make sure they retain their shape when used in cookies.

Multiply any cake or bar recipe that fits in a 9 x 13-inch pan by 1.5 to fit in a half-sheet pan. Baking times may be adjusted accordingly - perhaps increased by 5 minutes or so.

Rescue slightly over-whipped whipped cream? Yes. If you started with 1 cup, stir in 1/4 cup additional heavy cream until the consistency returns to normal. If it's really, really over whipped (and you haven't added sugar) you can transfer it to a food processor and make butter instead.

Instead of granulated sugar, I usually add confectioners' sugar to whipped cream. It adds a measure of stability and naturally holds up longer.

Keep a 12-inch ruler in the kitchen drawer - you'll be amazed how many times it will answer questions about pastry sizes and thickness of your biscuits.

To zest fruit peel efficiently, hold a microplane rasp in one hand and fruit in the other. Move the rasp on top of the fruit. The right-side-up position will catch the zest, and make it easy to measure.

COOKING with MORE CONFIDENCE

Salvia officinalis

(pineapple)

Common Weights and Measures

¼ cup = **4 tablespoons** = 2 fluid ounces

1/3 cup = **5 tablespoons + 1 teaspoon** = 2 ½ fluid ounces

½ cup = **8 tablespoons** = 4 fluid ounces

2/3 cup = **10 tablespoons + 2 teaspoons** = 5 fluid ounces

¾ cup = **12 tablespoons** = 8 fluid ounces

1 cup = **16 tablespoons** = 8 fluid ounces

1 pint = **2 cups** = 16 fluid ounces

1 quart = **4 cups** = 32 fluid ounces

Roasting Chart

BEEF
Internal Temperature Rare 120, Medium Rare 130, Medium 140
All cuts: Rest, loosely covered with foil, for 20 minutes before carving
Tenderloin: Roasting Temperature 450 degrees
Top loin, Strip Roast, Rib Roast: Roasting Temperature 350 degrees

PORK
Internal Temperature 155 Medium Well
Tenderloin: Roasting Temperature 400 degrees, Resting Time 5 minutes
Boneless loin: Roasting Temperature 350 degrees, Resting Time 20 minutes

POULTRY
Internal Temperature 180 degrees
Roasting Temperature 350 degrees

COOKING WITH MORE CONFIDENCE

How Much to Buy

Item	Amount to Buy	For Prepared Amount
Asparagus	1 pound fresh (12 to 20 spears)	3 1/2 cups chopped
Bacon	8 slices	1/2 cup crumbled
Bell Pepper	1 large	1 cup chopped
Broccoli	1 pound fresh	3 1/2 cups florets
Cabbage	1 small head (1 pound)	5 cups shredded
Celery	1 medium stalk	1/2 cup sliced
Green Onions	1 bunch	1/2 cup sliced
Herbs, fresh	1 Tablespoon	1 teaspoon dried
Mushrooms	8 ounces	2 cups chopped
Pasta	8 ounces	4-5 cups cooked
Potatoes	1 pound	3 1/2 - 4 cups chopped 2 cups mashed
Rice	1 cup raw long grain white rice	3 cups cooked
Tomato	1 medium	1 cup chopped

Emergency Substitutions

Ingredient	Substitution
1 teaspoon baking powder	¼ teaspoon baking soda + 5/8 teaspoon cream of tartar
1 cup buttermilk	1 tablespoon lemon juice + enough milk to equal 1 cup. Let stand 5 minutes before using.
1 ounce unsweetened chocolate	3 tablespoons unsweetened cocoa powder + 1 tablespoon melted butter
1 ounce semisweet chocolate	½ ounce unsweetened chocolate + 1 tablespoon granulated sugar
6 ounces melted semisweet chocolate	½ cup + 1 tablespoon cocoa powder + ¼ cup + 3 tablespoons granulated sugar + 3 tablespoons butter
1 cup heavy cream	1/3 cup melted butter + ¾ cup milk
1 cup sour cream	1 tablespoon lemon juice + enough evaporated whole milk to equal 1 cup
1 tablespoon espresso coffee powder	1 ½ tablespoon instant coffee powder. The flavor won't be as intense, but will serve the purpose.
1 small clove garlic	1/8 teaspoon garlic powder
1 ½ teaspoons fresh herbs	½ teaspoon dried herbs. Exception? Rosemary. Use equal amounts of fresh to dry.
1 cup ketchup	1 cup tomato sauce + 2 tablespoons granulated sugar + 1 tablespoon vinegar
1 teaspoon prepared mustard	¼ teaspoon dried mustard + ¾ teaspoon vinegar
1 teaspoon dry mustard	1 tablespoon prepared mustard
1 cup confectioners' sugar	1 cup granulated sugar + 1 tablespoon cornstarch, pulsed a few seconds in a blender or food processor
1 cup light brown sugar	1 cup granulated sugar + 2 tablespoons molasses
1 cup dark brown sugar	1 cup granulated sugar + 3 tablespoons molasses
1 cup tomato sauce	½ cup tomato paste + ½ cup water

Index

Index

COOKING WITH MORE CONFIDENCE

Index

Index

Index

About the Author

Eunice Naomi Wiebolt was born and raised in Minnesota. Although immersed in the world of retail business in earlier years, she has always maintained a passionate interest in cooking and entertaining, as well as recipe research and development. Her culinary background includes training at Ecole De Gastronomie Francaise, Ritz-Escoffier, in Paris and the Santa Fe School of Cooking, among others.

Eunice attended college as a non traditional student. She holds an Associate in Arts degree with honors from Central Lakes College in Brainerd, Minnesota, and a Bachelor of Science degree in Vocational Education and Business from Bemidji State University in Bemidji, Minnesota.

Over the years, she has taught many cooking, business, career, and art classes in private, college, and business settings. Her earlier careers included ownership and management of an art and craft retail shop and a full service floral shop. She is a floral design school graduate and Master Florist.

Eunice remains active in the community as a member of a government commission, two local service organizations, a writers' group, and a book club. She is also a member of the Independent Book Publishers Association, Midwest Independent Publishing Association, and the Nature Printing Society.

Eunice enjoys her blended family of five sons and their families. She resides in the Brainerd Lakes area of northern Minnesota.

COOKING with MORE CONFIDENCE

COOKING WITH MORE CONFIDENCE
- AND -
COOKING WITH CONFIDENCE

<u>Cookbook Order Form</u>

Your Name   _____

Street   _____

City, State, Zip   _____

Ship To   _____

Street   _____

City, State, Zip   _____

<u>METHOD OF PAYMENT</u>

_____   Check   (Payable to Romarin Publishing Co.)

_____   Credit Card: Master Card _____   Visa _____

Name as it appears on the card   _____

Card number   _____ Exp. Date _____

Signature   _____

	Quantity	Amount Due
COOKING with MORE CONFIDENCE @ $26.95 each	_____	$_____
COOKING with CONFIDENCE @ $26.95 each	_____	$_____
Canada (added cost) @ $15.00 each	_____	$_____
Minnesota and Local Sales Tax ($2.00 per book)		$_____
Shipping and Handling ($5.00 per book)		$_____
Total		$_____

For volume purchases, email romarin@scicable.com

Please complete this form and return to:
Romarin Publishing Co.
1945 Red Oak Drive SW, Brainerd, MN 56401-2050
romarin@scicable.com